After 2,000 years Jesus remains the most influential leader in the history of the human race. He has changed family life like no other. In this wonderful book, Ken Blanchard along with Phil Hodges and Tricia Goyer show how Jesus can change *your* family to make it a life-giving, heart-expanding, soul-forming community of greatness.

—JOHN ORTBERG

Senior Pastor, Menlo Park Presbyterian Church; author of *Who Is This Man?*

If I were asked to pick only one book that would be required reading for every Christ-centered family, it would be this one. *Lead Your Family Like Jesus* is not only a game-changer, but a family-changer.

—TOMMY SPAULDING

The New York Times bestselling author of *It's Not Just Who You Know*

I wish I'd had the simple but powerful and persuasive insights offered by Ken, Phil, and Tricia in *Lead Your Family Like Jesus* when I was raising my son. Nonetheless, because I am convinced that they "nailed" it with this magnificent offering, I intend to purchase several copies of this gem in order to share it with my young mentees as they begin their parenting years. Frankly, I suspect it will be considered their favorite gift of the new year.

—COLLEEN BARRETT

President Emeritus, Southwest Airlines Co.

Ken Blanchard has spent his lifetime studying leadership. *Lead Your Family Like Jesus* is a fresh and original approach to leadership. Filled with practical parables and good advice, this is a book worth reading.

—BOB BUFORD

Author, *Halftime* and *Finishing Well*

There is no greater leadership charge than the one God gives us to influence the thinking, behavior, and development of our children. It's through our life role leadership we are positioned to teach our children how to reflect the heart and beauty of Christ in the world. *Lead Your Family Like Jesus* illuminates the example of Jesus and provides all the wisdom parents need to raise up Christ-centered servant leaders. Every parent *must* read this book to understand how to steward well the sacred trust they've been given.

—TAMI HEIM

President and CEO, Christian Leadership Alliance

I wish this book was available twenty-two years ago when our first child was born. It would have been the best baby shower gift ever given. I know what gift I'm giving to all new parents!

—DINA DWYER-OWENS
   Chairwoman and CEO, The Dwyer Group; mother of Dani and Mikey

As a pastor, I'm always looking for helpful and practical resources for families. *Lead Your Family Like Jesus* is phenomenal. The twelve principles presented in this incredible read are wise, biblical, encouraging, and transforming. It's rare to find one book with so many relational gems. The best part is that these grace-filled truths are applicable to every family situation. I have been a Blanchard and Hodges fan for years; this book is one of their best!

—KURT BUBNA
   Lead Pastor, Eastpoint Church, Spokane Valley, Washington

In very relatable ways, *Lead Your Family Like Jesus* takes readers on an engaging ride into the heart of what the Lord asks of us as parents. With Ken, Phil, and Trish being so vulnerable with their own stories—woven around both Scripture and sharing from other parents with similar challenges and triumphs—I felt like I was right there, parenting alongside them. This is a must-read for moms and dads looking for real-life encouragement to be an even better version of themselves—the version God is calling them to be!

—JIM HAUSKEY
   Marketing Director, DaySpring

Lead Your Family Like Jesus is a book that deserves a prominent place on every family's bookshelf. Engaging from the first page, each chapter shares unique, valuable insight from the authors. As a mother and grandmother, I discovered new ways to put essential biblical principles of leading into action—and I'm already seeing results. No matter where you are in life, *Lead Your Family Like Jesus* meets you where you are today. Be prepared to refer to this wonderful volume time and time again!

—SHERRY GORE
   Editor-in-chief, *Cooking & Such* magazine

Ken and Phil, and this time with Tricia Goyer, have done it again! Their new book, *Lead Your Family Like Jesus*, is incredible. It is a must read for all parents of every age.

—JIM BLANCHARD
   Chairman of the Board, Jordan-Blanchard Capital, LLC

KEN BLANCHARD
PHIL HODGES
& TRICIA GOYER

LEAD
YOUR FAMILY
LIKE JESUS

POWERFUL PARENTING PRINCIPLES
FROM THE CREATOR OF FAMILIES

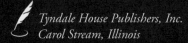

Tyndale House Publishers, Inc.
Carol Stream, Illinois

Lead Your Family Like Jesus

Copyright © 2013 by The Center for Faithwalk Leadership/Lead Like Jesus
All rights reserved.

A Focus on the Family book published by Tyndale House Publishers, Carol Stream, Illinois 60188

Focus on the Family and the accompanying logo and design are federally registered trademarks
of Focus on the Family, Colorado Springs, CO 80995.

TYNDALE is a registered trademark of Tyndale House Publishers, Inc. Tyndale's quill logo is a
trademark of Tyndale House Publishers, Inc.

All Scripture quotations, unless otherwise indicated, are taken from the *Holy Bible, New Interna-
tional Version®*. NIV®. Copyright © 1973, 1978, 1984 by Biblica, Inc.™ Used by permission of
Zondervan. All rights reserved worldwide. (www.zondervan.com). Scripture quotations marked
(MSG) are taken from *The Message* [paraphrase]. Copyright © by Eugene H. Peterson 1993, 1994,
1995, 1996, 2000, 2001, 2002. Used by permission of NavPress Publishing Group. Scripture
quotations marked (NASB) are taken from the *New American Standard Bible®*. Copyright © 1960,
1962, 1963, 1968, 1971, 1972, 1973, 1975, 1977, 1995 by The Lockman Foundation. Used by
permission. (www.Lockman.org). Scripture quotations marked (KJV) are taken from the *King
James Version*. Scripture quotations marked (ESV) are from *The Holy Bible, English Standard
Version®*, (ESV®), copyright © 2001 by Crossway, a publishing ministry of Good News
Publishers. Used by permission. All rights reserved. Scripture quotations identified as being taken
from *The Living Bible* [paraphrase], copyright © 1971 by Tyndale House Foundation, are used by
permission of Tyndale House Publishers, Inc., Carol Stream, Illinois 60188. All rights reserved.

Cover design: Rule 29
Phil Hodges photo by Paul Pinner
Tricia Goyer photo by Jessica McCollam
Ken Blanchard photo © The Ken Blanchard Companies
"Edging God Out" and "Exalting God Only" diagrams © 2002 by The Center for Faithwalk
Leadership/Lead Like Jesus; "Learning Stages" diagram © 2005 by The Center for Faithwalk
Leadership/Lead Like Jesus. All rights reserved.
The use of material from or references to various Web sites does not imply endorsement of those
sites in their entirety.

Library of Congress Cataloging-in-Publication Data pending

ISBN 978-1-58997-720-4 (alk. paper)

Printed in the United States of America
1 2 3 4 5 6 7 / 19 18 17 16 15 14 13

To all parents everywhere
who quietly go about the work of
pouring their lives and unconditional love
into the hearts of their children.

CONTENTS

ACKNOWLEDGMENTS

In appreciation and gratitude to the following people who played an important role in bringing *Lead Your Family Like Jesus* to life:

Janet Kobobel Grant for her work as literary agent on behalf of this project.

Phyllis Hendry for her enthusiasm and support as well as her leadership in managing the details of the agreement needed for this book to be published.

Martha Lawrence for loving attitude and artistry in editing the final pre-submission manuscript.

Thank you to the Focus on the Family and Tyndale teams for catching the vision for this project. Special thanks goes to Larry Weeden and John Duckworth for the fantastic work with our manuscript, and to everyone else who has done so much to get this book into the hands of parents. We appreciate you!

FROM PHIL:

Thank you to:

Karen McGuire for her friendship and wise advice in the development of the biblical components of the book.

Ed Lassiter, my fellow grandpa, for sharing his story of wisdom in guiding his son.

Susanne Kinnaird for being the image of a caring, listening mom.

My wife, Jane Kinnaird Hodges, for her love and practical wisdom as a devoted wife, mother, and grandmother.

My parents, Emile Philip Hodges and Elizabeth Cockburn Hodges, for the love, laughter, and practical optimism that filled our home and their marriage for sixty-three years.

My sister, Liz Hodges Pavoni, for filling in the blanks about the stories of our childhood.

Jane's parents, Eugene and Jean Kinnaird, as models of faith in Christ and commitment to one another, their children, and extended family for all seventy-one years of their marriage.

Our son, Phil; his wife, Marion Hodges; our daughter, LeeAnne; and her husband, Paul Pinner, for stories from their daily service and sacrifice as the loving parents of Julia, Philip, John, Sarah, James, Samuel, and Andrew.

Most of all I want to thank God and His Son, Jesus Christ, for the gift of love and family.

FROM TRICIA:

Thank you to Amy Lathrop and the Litfuze Hens for supporting me and helping me stay connected with my readers.

I appreciate my friends Skyler and Tara letting me share "our" story.

Thank you, Ocieanna Fleiss, for letting me share your life-saving, life-changing story. I'm so thankful you've had more time with us on this earth.

John, you had no idea that an 18-year-old single mom would become a multi-published author, did you? I'm thankful to share this parenting journey with you.

Thanks to our children—Cory, Leslie, Nathan, and Alyssa, and my daughter-in-law as well as grandson Clayton. What joy you bring to our lives!

A special thanks to Grandma Dolores. I am blessed that you live with us and I get to share daily life with you. And to my parents, who showed me so much about the world and about the love of a family.

A special thanks goes to all the parents who provided their transparent insight for this book: Martha, Allison, Regina, Heather, Haelie, Dori, Sami, Paige, Joanne, Beth, Tommy, Wendy, Brett, Joey, Robin, Danielle, Betsy, Michelle, Christy, Fernanda, Kennisha, Jayna, Diane, Caren, Caroline, Amy, and Jennifer. We appreciate your taking time to answer our questions, give input, and share your heart!

Finally, to my best Friend, Jesus Christ: None of this would be possible without You. When I prayed, "If You can do anything with my life, please do," You took that prayer seriously. You've done more than I could ever ask for or imagine!

FROM KEN:

Thanks to my team at The Ken Blanchard Companies:

Margery Allen, my right and left hand, for her sense of humor that keeps me sane.

Martha Lawrence, for her loving support and ability to make my writing come alive.

Renee Broadwell, Martha's and my writing partner, who's always ready to lend a hand.

And last but not least, Anna Espino, who epitomizes a servant heart— always ready to help in any way.

Thanks also to my dad, Ted Blanchard, and my mom, Dorothy Blanchard, for always being there as parents—making me feel special and capable of doing anything I ever set my mind to.

To my son, Scott, and daughter, Debbie, who have smiled and forgiven me for telling stories about them. I am also proud of Scott for being a great dad to Kurtis and Kyle and proud of Debbie for being a great mom to Alec.

To Madeleine Homan Blanchard, for her love and devotion to my newest grandkids, Hanna and Atticus—young adults I am proud of in every way.

To my best friend and partner of fifty years, Margie, for being a parent extraordinaire as well as a great business partner. I feel blessed to have you in my life as well as your wonderful McKee family—especially your brother, Tom, his fabulous wife, Jill, and their terrific kids, Julie and Casey.

Finally, to my long-term friend Phil Hodges, who inspired me to open my heart to Jesus. As a result, I am not only forgiven for my past and guaranteed my future, but I'm also blessed to have Him with me every day the rest of my life. Thanks, Phil, for helping me realize that Jesus is the greatest leadership role model—not only for how to lead at work, but also for how to lead at home.

To Lead Is to Serve

What person—living or dead—has most influenced your thinking, behavior, and path in life? Was it your mother? Your father? A coach? A teacher?

The person you just named was a leader in your life, regardless of his or her formal title. If, as most people do, you named a family member or friend, you can see that leaders with titles and positions of authority make up only part of the leadership landscape.

Why? Because leadership is an influence process. In fact:

> *Any time you seek to influence the thinking,*
> *behavior, or development of another person,*
> *you take on the role of a leader.*

When you think about it this way, all of us are leaders in every aspect of life. That is why most leadership that shapes us doesn't come from those with boxes on an organizational chart; it comes from those we encounter in everyday life. That's where our focus will be in this book: on your role as a leader in your family. The truth is, being a parent is probably the most important life-role leadership position you'll ever have, and it begins when you assume responsibility for raising a child. Yet most people have no training or framework to help them be the best parents possible.

This book is here to help change that. We'll show how the example and teachings of Jesus two thousand years ago apply to the busy lives of ordinary moms and dads today. By looking at Jesus, you can learn how to build a loving relationship with your children and extended family—no matter how you were raised and no matter what challenges your family faces.

Those challenges are all around us. In too many families love has been distorted to "you don't love me unless you [fill in the blank]," rather than the unconditional loving that Jesus modeled. Self-promotion (pride) and self-protection (fear) have replaced love and vulnerability. We're afraid to give our whole hearts to others because we don't want to be hurt. Indifference moves in and intimacy is replaced with isolation.

The good news is that there's a better way. There's a perfect leadership role model you can trust. His name is Jesus. All families matter to Him. The big question is, does Jesus matter in your family? We'll be exploring this question with you throughout the book.

When Jesus used a towel and basin to wash the disciples' feet (John 13:1-17), He modeled leadership as an act of service. Service means thinking of others before ourselves. It means giving rather than receiving.

Two people who exemplified servant leadership in the life of Jesus were His mother, Mary, and His stepfather, Joseph.

Mary had no material wealth, yet she was rich with a servant's heart. She responded to the call to become the earthly parent of the Savior by saying, "I am the Lord's servant. . . . May it be to me as you have said" (Luke 1:38). With that declaration she set the highest standard for a heart surrendered for service. In her life-role as a mother, Mary was positioned to have major influence on her child. The relationship between a serving mother and son was part of God's plan of preparation for Jesus' own season of earthly leadership. Mary passed on to her son important lessons about obedience, submission, faith, and service.

Joseph overcame all the pride and fear issues involved in accepting Mary as his wife and Jesus as his child to rear. Although the Bible does not record anything Joseph said, his actions—providing for the physical and spiritual well-being of his family—display the nature of his heart.

The book of Luke sums up the combined results of these humble, faith-centered parents:

> *Then he [Jesus] went down to Nazareth with*
> *them [Mary and Joseph] and was obedient*
> *to them. . . . And Jesus grew in wisdom and stature,*
> *and in favor with God and men. (Luke 2:51-52)*

God tested Mary and Joseph and found the hearts of servants. No wonder He chose His Son to be raised by such parents.

God has gifted you with your children. Will you nurture them with a servant heart, as Mary and Joseph nurtured Jesus?

LEADING IS SERVING

What does leading with a servant heart look like in a family? Imagine the following situations; each describes someone engaged in an act of family leadership.

- A mother caring for a child during the day
- A father listening to his children's nighttime prayers
- Parents helping a teenager walk through unplanned pregnancy
- A husband and wife modeling their faith in God in the face of the loss of a job
- An adult son providing guidance on living arrangements for his aging parents
- A terminally ill sibling showing grace, confidence, courage, and calm to anxious loved ones

These family leaders are making personal choices about how and to what end they will use their influence. When it comes to decisions like these, each of us must decide:

Am I seeking to serve God and the well-being of my family members, or am I seeking my own self-interest?

When parents lead like Jesus, they serve God and others with love as the ultimate goal. As a result, children gain character-building skills and self-worth, and family relationships thrive!

THE FOUR DOMAINS

Leading your family like Jesus, you learn to align four leadership domains: your heart, your head, your hands, and your habits.

Heart: *The character and the values* you employ as you lead and influence your children.

Head: *Your viewpoint and beliefs* about leading and influencing your children.

Hands: *What you actually do* when leading and influencing your children.

Habits: *How you continually refocus your desire* to lead and influence your children as Jesus would have you do.

When these areas align, leading becomes a joy—and you and your family experience feelings of safety, security, and satisfaction. When these areas are out of alignment, dissatisfaction and distrust result. In the following pages we'll discuss how these domains get out of whack and how to bring them back into alignment—something we all need from time to time!

OUR STORIES

I'm delighted that Phil Hodges and Tricia Goyer have joined me in discussing how to lead like Jesus in the family. Phil was the coauthor of the original *Lead*

Like Jesus book. A grandfather *par excellence*, he has been a dear friend for more than fifty years. Tricia Goyer is the award-winning author of hundreds of articles and dozens of books on Christian themes. As a mom—and one-time unwed mother—she brings an important perspective to this subject.

My experience in leading a family with my wife, Margie, spans fifty years. Phil and Jane have celebrated their forty-fifth anniversary. Contrast this with Tricia and John, who have celebrated twenty-three years of marriage. We hope that the three of us, sharing from our unique viewpoints, can give you a well-rounded picture of what it looks like when we let Jesus guide our families.

We also hope that in reading this book you'll experience Jesus in a new and different way. As you read our stories and see these principles in action, we believe you'll grow to trust Jesus as the perfect role model to follow. But this can happen only if you surrender all of your life—even your family life—to Him. It's easier said than done, but this is the key:

> *Trust in the Lord with all your heart and lean not on your*
> *own understanding; in all your ways acknowledge him,*
> *and he will make your paths straight.(Proverbs 3:5-6)*

Lead Your Family Like Jesus will help you take Christ out of the separate compartment of your private spiritual life and give Him free rein in all your daily actions and relationships. It's not a textbook, but rather a collection of stories and advice about how we let Jesus guide our attitudes, actions, and behaviors in our families—sometimes with miraculous results.

We've divided the book into twelve chapters. Phil, Tricia, and I will take turns discussing different aspects of the heart, head, hands, and habits of leading your family like Jesus. We've also included the input of other parents, allowing them to share their triumphs and struggles. I hope you'll enjoy these stories and through them see how leading like Jesus can bring limitless blessings to your family.

—Ken Blanchard

Coauthor, *The One Minute Manager*® and *Lead Like Jesus*

PART I

THE HEART

Leading like Jesus as a parent is first a spiritual matter.

Whenever you have an opportunity to influence the thinking and behavior of other family members, the first question you have to answer is, "Am I motivated by self-interest or by the betterment of those I'm leading?"

The answer to that question starts on the inside; it's a heart issue. If you don't get the heart right, you simply won't become a parent who leads like Jesus.

In Part I, Ken shows how a disaster gave him the long-term perspective Jesus has—and that every parent needs. Phil explains how an unChristlike kind of EGO—Edging God Out—causes us to make choices that hurt our families. Tricia describes how we can do the opposite with another kind of EGO—Exalting God Only—a pattern Jesus set.

ONE

Important Forever

PRINCIPLE 1

To Lead Like Jesus, Have an Eternal Perspective

Through His words and actions, Jesus taught that what people carry in their hearts is far more important than what they wear on their backs or where they lay their heads. He knew our hearts would be where our treasures are (Matthew 6:21). In his story about a major loss, Ken describes how he learned to take the long view—and how that view can revolutionize your parenting.

The voice message came when Margie and I were in Florida on an October day in 2007. She was at a conference in Orlando; I was in Naples playing golf with a bunch of old Cornell buddies. I got up a bit before 7:00 and checked my cell phone for messages. There was only one. It was from our son, Scott:

"Mom, Dad, I don't know where you are, but Mad and I had to evacuate our house. When we got down the road, we looked up and there were flames coming out of our place, and I think yours is gone, too. It's just awful."

That was my greeting for the day. The San Diego fires—which we'd last heard were thirty-five miles from our home—had reached our doorstep. It looked as if they'd consumed it.

Frankly, Margie and I were sadder for our son than we were for ourselves. Scott and his wife, Madeleine, had just finished a ten-month remodel of their house. They'd done it with such love and care, and had just moved in. They'd created a happy home for their family.

Margie and I prayed. We asked God that if one house could be spared, it would be theirs.

Next day I was driving with my friend and coauthor Phil Hodges when I got the call from Scott.

"Dad, you won't believe it!" he shouted. "I'm standing in our living room and our house was saved!"

Our prayer had been answered! The front doormat and some towels on the back deck had been charred—and the houses on both sides had burned to the ground. But Scott and Madeleine's house had been spared.

Scott's tone turned serious. "I'm afraid your house is gone, Dad."

"Scott, that's exactly what Mom and I prayed would happen!" I shouted, laughing and crying with happiness.

It mattered less that our house was gone. I was so overjoyed by Scott's news that we pulled the car over by the beach. Phil and I got out and ran along the shore shouting, "Lord, You're unbelievable!" Phil got a picture of me with my hands in the air and a great grin on my face.

Maybe my reaction was influenced by some reading I'd been doing. I'd just finished John Ortberg's wonderful book *When the Game Is Over, It All Goes Back in the Box*. John has a marvelous exercise in the book that goes like this:

It's 4:00 in the afternoon and you're getting ready to go home. There are two piles of Post-It notes on your desk. One says *Important Forever* and the other says *Temporary Stuff*. Put a Post-It from one of the two piles on everything you notice as you leave—the computer, your desk, your administrative assistant, the Coke machine, your receptionist, your car. Then do the same when you get home—on your bicycle, your golf clubs, people, and things in the house.

After the fire, it was clear to Margie and me where those sticky notes should go. What's really *Important Forever* is who you love and who loves you. We knew God was with us and what was really important in life, even as we walked through the ashes. Our family was safe. Even our dog was safe and being cared for by a friend. We'd lost a lot of temporary stuff, including many precious mementos, but we had each other. We still had our children, our grandchildren, our friends, and our coworkers.

Pause & Reflect

- What is the *Temporary Stuff* in your life? What is *Important Forever*?
- As a leader of your family, are you focusing on what's temporary—or on what will last?

WHAT DID JESUS DO?

Jesus knew all about that kind of eternal perspective:

> "Don't hoard treasure down here where it gets eaten by moths and corroded by rust or—worse!—stolen by burglars. Stockpile treasure in heaven, where it's safe from moth and rust and burglars. It's obvious, isn't it? The place where your treasure is, is the place you will most want to be, and end up being." (Matthew 6:19-21, MSG)

Just knowing about the long-term view wasn't enough for Jesus, of course. Everything He did was about the forever benefits, and He calls us to do the same:

> Do you see what this means—all these pioneers who blazed the way, all these veterans cheering us on? It means we'd better get on with it. Strip down, start running—and never quit! No extra spiritual fat, no parasitic sins. Keep your eyes on *Jesus*, who both began and finished this race we're in. Study how he did it. Because he never lost sight of where he was headed—that exhilarating finish in and with God—he could put up with anything along the way: cross, shame, whatever. And now he's *there*, in the place of honor, right alongside God. When you find yourselves

flagging in your faith, go over that story again, item by item, that long litany of hostility he plowed through. *That* will shoot adrenaline into your souls! (Hebrews 12:1-3, MSG)

HOLDING LOOSELY, CLINGING TIGHTLY

For many years Margie and I had a vision for our family, and those beliefs came out through our actions. We believed our house was not our own, that God had given it to us for His use. When we lost it, we mourned for the dwelling. But we also rejoiced in the ways God had allowed us to use it to care for others.

Because we wanted to celebrate all the good times, we held a memorial celebration for our house. The purpose of our service was to talk about the good times people had there. More than 100 people attended! Over the course of twenty-five years, individuals and families had lived in our home for two, three, or even more months. It was wonderful to have others talk about a party they remembered, or how they'd lived there during a tough time. They shared how it felt to be in our home. We immersed ourselves in what had been great about that house and all the memories we'd built there.

There are temporary things that always need to be done—cleaning, cooking, bathing, etc.—but I also like to focus on things that last forever, like spending time with others, serving others, making sure to praise my children, teaching them godly principles, and educating them.

—MARTHA, mother of four

At the end of that event, our daughter, Debbie—who has quite the sense of humor—spoke. "You know, I used to go to my parents' house," she said. "And I would look in the closets and the garage and would think, *When something happens to them, it's going to be my job to clean this all out!* And I don't have to do that now!"

Her comment may have seemed flippant, but in many ways it just reflected this reality: Even though our material things were gone, the memories were still with us. Our lives had been lightened. What we carried in our hearts was something that could never be taken away. And the service we gave to others in that house would forever be carried with them. No fire could destroy that.

CHERISHING THOSE YOU LOVE

It's easy to focus our time and efforts on things—jobs, houses, activities. But in times like the fire we learn that what we carry in our hearts and relationships is what lasts. Margie and I were challenged to hold things loosely and cherish people—particularly our family and one another. We were reminded that God's love is another thing that lasts; a fire can't take it away.

Peter Drucker once said that nothing good ever happens by accident. If you want something good to happen, he advised, put some structure around it. So let me give you some practical ways to act on the eternal perspective by cherishing your family. We have a few traditions that might inspire you.

Birthday Blessings. On every family member's birthday, we have a family gathering. As part of the celebration, we sit at the dining room table. One by one, each of us tells the person whose birthday it is what we really love and cherish about him or her. Our kids, Scott and Debbie, used to protest this tradition. But today they encourage their kids to take part in it, too.

Christmas Recital. Between dinner and dessert on Christmas Day, all our family and friends who are gathered share something special with everyone. They can sing a song, recite a poem, or tell us something important in their lives. This not only delights all those who are gathered, it makes the day memorable and meaningful.

Date Night. Margie's brother, Tom, and his wife, Jill, try to schedule a date night every week, when they get a babysitter and have a night just for themselves. There is no focus on their work or kids, just on their relationship. What a wonderful way to cherish each other!

Our Christmas Eve tradition started when our daughter was ten months old. It includes my husband reading the Christmas story from our family Bible while [we drink] hot chocolate. We also read a version of "The Night Before Christmas." As the kids have gotten older, they want to read the story from the Bible. We look forward to it every year!

—Regina, mother of two

My husband and I are very intentional about having a weekly (almost always) date night. Our kids know that it is a time for the two of us. Our eldest also has seen that we take time for our marriage by going to marriage conferences to keep "tuned up." Our whole household tells each other "I love you" whenever we are leaving. We want the last thing heard from us to be something kind and "forever," in case Jesus takes us home before we see each other again.

—Allison, mom of three

ETERNAL LIFE, ABUNDANT LIFE

You may be thinking, *Was having your house burn to the ground really such a positive experience? It's nice that you learned a lesson, but didn't you have at least a little trouble with this disaster?*

Of course we did. And dealing with it meant taking a more eternal, God-centered perspective, too. As I tried to process the loss of our house and all our things, I thought of one of my favorite Bible verses:

> **"I came that they may have life and that they may have it abundantly." (John 10:10, ESV)**

Just before the fire, I'd been studying another John passage with my Bible teacher and friend, Rich Case:

*"I am the vine; you are the branches. If a man remains
in me and I in him, he will bear much fruit; apart
from me you can do nothing." (John 15:5)*

During this study I'd asked Rich, "What did Jesus mean by abundant life?"

"Jesus wants us to have joy, peace, and righteousness," Rich had said. "Any time you don't feel joyful or peaceful or right with God, you're probably going it your own way and you're detached from the vine."

As the reality of losing our home and everything in it sank in, Margie and I weren't very joyful or peaceful. After I shared with Margie what I'd learned from Rich, we put our hands out and said, "Lord, we really need You. We can't make it through this by ourselves." With that thought constantly in our minds, we were able to maintain a peaceful feeling in the days and weeks that followed. Jesus met us in our time of need.

And that's the key to leading a family like Jesus—not only following His example, but relying on His presence within us. It's our lives connected to His.

We parents can try to give and serve in our own strength, but we won't get very far. It's His heart we're striving for. When we find His heart, He will transform ours. We can turn to Him during the hardest times of family life, and He'll be there, giving us the peace to make it through—and reminding us what's most important.

I have three kids. One has Asperger's and the other two are strong-willed. It is a necessity that I ask Jesus to walk with me. So each morning before my feet touch the floor, I pray. I ask Jesus to be tangible, to help me be able to hear His voice over the chaos that sometimes swallows my day.

—HEATHER, *mother of three*

We aim—though we often fail—to include Christ in every aspect of our daily living. I pray first thing in the morning. My wife and son read the

Bible together during home preschool time. We pray at meals—not just as a routine, but with intentional hearts together as a family. We pray when we need help and we try to remember to praise as quickly as we can. As a family, we know we need Him, and we're trying to work together to remind each other to go to Him first. We end our day together as a family, reading our "goodnight" books and Scripture.

—JOEY, father of two

When we lost our house, in the world's eyes we'd lost everything—but Margie and I knew better. We'd spent twenty-five years caring for the things in our home. In the end, Margie and I—and the family we built—are what stood. That's what the foundation of leading your family like Jesus is all about: focusing on who you love and who loves you.

Leading your family like Jesus focuses on what's really important.

And it all starts in the heart.

Pause & Reflect

- Tonight, thank God for giving you a family and a chance to parent.
- Write a prayer telling God you're a willing servant for your family. As you're preparing that prayer, do an honest assessment of how often you're a servant leader in your family—and how often you're a self-serving leader.

TWO

Say No to EGO

PRINCIPLE 2

To Lead Like Jesus, Be Humble

Our decisions and responsibilities as family leaders can feel overwhelming. In this story of pride and fear gone wrong, Phil illustrates what can happen when we're too proud to rely on God's guidance to manage our homes—and how to break that pattern.

"The righter she sounded, the madder I got."

That's the best way to describe what happened whenever my wife, Jane, and I spoke about the failing investment I'd poured our funds into when our kids were young. In my heart of hearts, I'd suspected I didn't know what I was doing when I got into the investment game. I must admit that, in addition to providing financial security for our family, I wanted to show Jane and our friends that I was a player in the game of wise investing.

In his book *The Search for Significance*, Robert S. McGee noted that if Satan has a formula for self-worth, it includes buying into this idea: "Your self-worth equals your performance plus the opinion of others." This certainly could be applied to my attitude regarding my investment.

When the deal started to sour, trying to save it required additional money. I bullied Jane into committing more funds, instead of confronting my own loss of self-esteem and fear of failure.

I often find myself overwhelmed with life's struggles, and in those times my natural instinct is to try to figure everything out and fix it myself. I am often afraid that if I don't take care of it myself, then it will all come crumbling down. Also, I often see my struggles as deserved by me because of poor decisions on my part, so in that way I tend to see them as my responsibility to endure and fix if at all possible.

If and when I get caught up in this self-reliance and prideful, fearful thinking, I am so thankful that God usually snaps me out of it and forces my focus back to Him. It is amazing and indescribable how He quickly and faithfully gives me His peace that passes all understanding as well as His strength and endurance.

—HAELIE, mother of one

After months of avoiding this landmine subject, Jane finally asked me if I'd prayed about it. My quick answer: "No!"

She then asked a second question that stopped me in my tracks. "Why not?"

Even though I'd been raised in a Christian home and continued to attend church regularly, it took me time to figure out the answer to Jane's question. Finally I realized three reasons I hadn't prayed about my finances.

First, it didn't seem right to bother God with my investment problems. They seemed so trivial compared to the kinds of things I thought were worthy of calling to God's attention, like a major illness or global problems such as the AIDS pandemic or the plight of innocent victims of natural disasters and wars.

Second, I didn't pray because I didn't have a lot of faith in the process. The best way to describe my concept of prayer at the time was that it was like tying my requests onto strings of helium balloons and letting them go. I had little confidence they'd ever be answered.

Third, I told myself I didn't need to pray because I could take care of the problem myself. Belief in God and in Jesus Christ had always been part of my life, but I'd let my pride, self-promotion, fear, and self-protection edge God out as the source of my security and sufficiency. I'd isolated myself from His help.

You might say I had an EGO problem—with EGO standing for Edging God Out.

If I'd made a diagram explaining that problem, here's what it might have looked like:

EDGING GOD OUT AS

Whom I worship
My source of security and self-worth
My audience, my ultimate authority, and my Judge

Pride

An overly high opinion of yourself, exaggerated esteem of self, haughtiness, arrogance

"Do not think of yourself more highly than you ought."
Romans 12:3

Fear

An insecure view of the future producing self-protection.

"Fear of man is a dangerous trap . . ."
Proverbs 29:25 (TLB)

Promoting Self

• Boasting
• Taking all the credit
• Showing off
• Doing all the talking
• Demanding all the attention

Protecting Self

• Hiding behind position
• Withholding information
• Intimidating others
• Hoarding control and revenues
• Discouraging honest feedback

Always separates
man from God, other people, and himself or herself

Always compares
with others and is never happy

Always distorts
the truth into a false sense of security or fear

Pause & Reflect

- As a parent, how do you tend to let your pride and fear edge God out as the source of your security and sufficiency?
- Which part of the diagram reminds you most of yourself? Why?

FROM PRIDE TO PEACE

When my investments were failing, I felt defeated—and isolated from my wife and children. At this low point in my life, God showed up in the pages of an unlikely book.

One Sunday morning I stayed home while Jane and the kids went off to church. Lying in bed, I started looking idly through a section of a book that Jane had suggested I read. It had a pretty macho title: *Disciplines of the Beautiful Woman.*

As I skimmed the pages of this book by Anne Ortlund, I came across a Bible quotation:

> *Do not be anxious about anything, but in everything,*
> *by prayer and petition, with thanksgiving, present your*
> *requests to God. And the peace of God, which transcends*
> *all understanding, will guard your hearts and your*
> *minds in Christ Jesus. (Philippians 4:6-7)*

I suppose I'd read these words before—without effect. This time they hit me right between the eyes. The one that drilled right into my soul was "anything." In an instant I realized that there was nothing that troubled me that God didn't want to hear about. That included my shaky investment. I was convinced that He would answer my prayer, no matter how puny it was.

So I rolled out of bed, humbled myself, got on my knees, and talked to God about my problem. I asked Him for the peace He promised. With words of surrender I gave up my problem to God, and at that moment I experienced a feeling like warm water pouring down over my soul. I felt a peace that truly transcended all understanding, just as God had promised.

When Jane and the kids came home, she looked at me, bewildered. "What happened to you?" she asked.

I guess the change that God had made in my heart had started to show on my face.

This began the process by which I started leading my family in its faith journey. Jane had carried that responsibility for too long.

I wish I could tell you that the investment made a miraculous turnaround, and I was able to retire early on the proceeds. That didn't happen. I lost the money, but I also found something of far greater value. I found the peace that surpasses all understanding—through prayer and the promises of God.

As a man, I don't want to admit that I need anything outside of myself to survive. It's almost like I am admitting defeat or that I am weak if I have to depend on God for something. I was always taught that with hard work a man should be able to provide everything his family needs.

—Tommy, father of two

THE EXAMPLE OF JESUS

When it comes to humility, Jesus was truly the Master. You've probably heard about the time when, despite His heavenly credentials, He washed His followers' dirty feet:

> Jesus knew that the Father had put him in complete charge of every-
> thing, that he came from God and was on his way back to God. So he
> got up from the supper table, set aside his robe, and put on an apron.
> Then he poured water into a basin and began to wash the feet of the

disciples, drying them with his apron. When he got to Simon Peter, Peter said, "Master, *you* wash *my* feet?"

Jesus answered, "You don't understand now what I'm doing, but it will be clear enough to you later."

Peter persisted, "You're not going to wash my feet—ever!"

Jesus said, "If I don't wash you, you can't be part of what I'm doing.". . .

After he had finished washing their feet, he took his robe, put it back on, and went back to his place at the table.

Then he said, "Do you understand what I have done to you? You address me as 'Teacher' and 'Master,' and rightly so. That is what I am. So if I, the Master and Teacher, washed your feet, you must now wash each other's feet. I've laid down a pattern for you. What I've done, you do. I'm only pointing out the obvious. A servant is not ranked above his master; an employee doesn't give orders to the employer. If you understand what I'm telling you, act like it—and live a blessed life." (John 13:3-9, 12-17, MSG)

That was hardly the only time Jesus displayed His humble spirit, however. Early in His ministry, He demonstrated His desire to please only the Father and to turn control of His life over to Him. Jesus made that choice public when He surrendered all to His Father and insisted that John baptize Him "to fulfill all righteousness" (Matthew 3:15).

Sometimes Jesus' desire to please the Father wasn't just a matter of doing something that others might have considered beneath their dignity. He demonstrated this dramatically when He went into the wilderness and was tempted by Satan:

For the third test, the Devil took him on the peak of a huge mountain. He gestured expansively, pointing out all the earth's kingdoms, how glorious they all were. Then he said, "They're yours—lock, stock, and barrel. Just go down on your knees and worship me, and they're yours."

Jesus' refusal was curt: "Beat it, Satan!" He backed his rebuke with a third quotation from Deuteronomy: "Worship the Lord your God, and only him. Serve him with absolute single-heartedness." (Matthew 4:8-10, MSG)

Jesus repeatedly affirmed *whose He was* and *who He was*. He determined that He would live by the mission His Father had given Him for the accomplishment of His Father's purpose. Jesus could have been prideful; He was the Son of God. He could have been fearful; all the powers of darkness were against Him. Instead, in all these situations, Jesus chose the will of His Father. He chose to lead by serving.

The Son of God doesn't have an EGO problem. Too often we do, suspecting we don't have all the answers as parents, but not wanting anyone—even God—to tell us what to do or how to live.

FIVE IDEAS FOR PROUD—AND FEARFUL—PARENTS

What can we do about our EGO problem and the resulting bad decisions that can harm our families? Here are five suggestions.

1. *Identify times when pride and fear are likely to pop up.* Both can stem from comparison; we're either comparing our kids to other kids, or comparing ourselves to other parents. Sometimes we even compare our "real selves" with the ideal person we want to be.

Think ahead to upcoming events that may bring out pride or fear. Think through how you'll handle each situation by trusting God.

Here's an example: the parent-teacher conference.

You may find yourself fearing your child isn't up to the level of other kids. Or you may find out your child is a top student—inflating your pride. Instead of attending with the possibility of either emotion taking the front seat, go expecting that your child will have areas that need improvement. Go with an open heart, willing to learn and grow as a parent.

How about other situations that might bring fear? Here are a few more:

- The playground, where your toddler can't keep up with the other kids
- The soccer game, where your son or daughter sits on the bench more than he or she plays
- The clinic, where the doctor is concerned about developmental delays

On the flip side, when are you most likely to be prideful? Consider your response to the following:

- When your child gets the best math score in class
- When his teammates always look to him to score the most goals
- When she's the talk of the talent show

Think of each of these opportunities as moments to turn to God for wisdom and strength. He can help you focus on Him—and what's best for your child—without your emotions taking the front seat. If possible, turn to your spouse to talk through, and pray about, your pride and fear. What might usually cause you to pull away from your spouse or child could be God's way of bringing you together!

2. *Remember whose you are and who you are.* To help you avoid pride and fear, you must answer two critical questions:

- Whose am I?
- Who am I?

The first question deals with choosing the primary authority and audience for your life. In other words, who are you trying to please? Leaders often demonstrate whose they are by how they define success. Many people think it has to do with earthly power and position, as well as the opinions of others.

You can state it any way you like, but Scripture teaches us that ultimately we're created to please God. There's no pride in that. In the family leadership arena, you first have to choose whether or not you will please God.

The second question—"Who am I?"—deals with your life purpose. Why did the Lord put you on earth? What does He want to do through you?

Scripture teaches that true success is the fulfillment of the life-mission God planned for you. It's that amazing. You have no need for pride or fear when success depends on your relationship with Christ and the level of control you let Him have. Are you willing to surrender all to Him and live as He would have you live—as a servant, rather than serving yourself?

3. *Take the "So That" test.* How can you know whether pride or fear is motivating your actions? Let's say you're considering enrolling your child in a private school. Weigh that decision using the "So That" test. State why you want to put your child in that school. For example, you might say, "We're looking at putting our child in private school *so that* he has a better education."

Now follow that train of thought four more times:

- "We want him to have a better education *so that* he'll do better on test scores."
- "We want him to do better on test scores *so that* he'll be more appealing to colleges."
- "We want him to be more appealing to colleges *so that* he'll get more scholarships."
- "We want him to get more scholarships *so that* we'll have less college tuition to pay."

Going through this process can help you identify some reasons you might not otherwise admit—like, "We're considering private school so that we'll be respected in our community" (pride), or "We want him to do better on test scores so that we won't look like failures to the other parents" (fear).

Of course, this only works if you're honest. If you find out that you're trying to satisfy your pride and fear, do you really want your decisions to be driven by those emotions?

4. *Give up control and let God be your guide.* The natural outcome of deciding to please God—as well as turning over control of your life to Him—is a transformed perspective. If you resist pleasing God or giving Him control, your gaze will remain inward and focused on self. If you live to please God and put Him in charge, your view will be transformed to one that's outward,

filled with God-given confidence—and that leads you to humility and a life of service.

As you surrender control, look to the Lord for guidance. In our fear of looking foolish, we often avoid seeking wisdom from others, including God. But as theologian Søren Kierkegaard remarked, "If you don't first seek the kingdom of God you will never seek it."

Follow the instructions we were taught as kids about crossing the street: "Stop, look, and listen!" Listen with an open mind to God and to those affected by your decisions. If I'd been more open to Jane's intuition regarding my investment adventure, my lesson in humility might not have been so costly. Listen to those who see things from a different point of view.

Seeking God's direction in family life is not only a built-in safeguard against dysfunction, it's a practical expression of worship that will keep you in the peace that transcends all understanding. It requires stopping to ask God for directions, looking for warning signs that you may be on a pride-and-fear EGO trip, and listening for His "still, small voice."

Edging God Out separates us from Him, from others, and from knowing the true selves He designed us to be. Instead, we need to invite God in and allow Him to work in and through us.

5. *Trust Him.* As Proverbs 3:5-6 says, "Trust in the Lord." When we take one step in doing what we know we should, the rest becomes easier as God takes our hand and guides us. As you can guess, pride and fear are *not* invited on the journey.

This is often easier said than done. But it's the *doing* that proves the *trusting.* It happens in family crises like these:

- When the bills appear bigger than your income, trust in God by acknowledging that He is your Provider. He will supply what you need—not always what you want. He promises to take care of His children.

- When the doctor says your child has a health problem, trust God by calling on Him as the ultimate Healer. Even as you seek medical advice, pray specifically through each step. Encourage and exhibit God-grounded confidence that, as Romans 8:28 says, God will work everything for good. Remember that God is Master of each moment and each molecule.

- When your child struggles in school, trust God by asking Him for help and "owning" your part of the solution. Keep your pride and fear out of the way by collaborating with teachers in serving the best interest of your child. See your child and yourself as works-in-progress, giving and receiving grace. Remember who, and whose, both of you are—and what Jesus pledged:

> "Has anyone by fussing in front of the mirror ever gotten taller by so much as an inch? All this time and money wasted on fashion—do you think it makes that much difference? Instead of looking at the fashions, walk out into the fields and look at the wildflowers. They never primp or shop, but have you ever seen color and design quite like it? The ten best-dressed men and women in the country look shabby alongside them.
>
> "If God gives such attention to the appearance of wildflowers—most of which are never even seen—don't you think he'll attend to you, take pride in you, do his best for you? What I'm trying to do here is to get you to relax, to not be so preoccupied with *getting*, so you can respond to God's *giving*. People who don't know God and the way he works fuss over these things, but you know both God and how he works. Steep your life in God-reality, God-initiative, God-provisions. Don't worry about missing out. You'll find all your everyday concerns will be met.
>
> "Give your entire attention to what God is doing right now, and don't get worked up about what may or may not happen tomorrow. God will help you deal with whatever hard things come up when the time comes." (Matthew 6:27-34, MSG)

TIME TO BREAK THE CYCLE

When we turn from Jesus' humble example and Edge God Out, the trickle-down effect on our children is profound. When pride and fear take possession of our hearts, the damage to our kids is long-lasting and far-reaching. In fact, walking away from God has been the root of dysfunction in families since the beginning of time.

Adam and Eve wanted to be like God. When they succumbed to the temptations of pride and fear, they ended up hiding in the bushes. Their firstborn child, Cain, also took matters into his own hands and killed his younger brother, Abel, in a fit of prideful anger.

As I found when my family investment plan collapsed, family leaders Edge God Out when they trust in something other than God's character and unconditional love as their source of security and self-worth. Prideful or fear-filled parents tend to be quick to judge, quick to take offense, quick to speak, and quick to push blame away and pull praise closer. They embrace what looks good in their eyes—even when, deep down, they know it's not right.

Imagine the peace in a home where humble parents, following the example of Jesus, take this advice to heart:

> *My dear brothers, take note of this: Everyone should be quick to listen, slow to speak and slow to become angry. (James 1:19)*

Edging God Out not only affects current family relationships and the character of the next generation, it will also influence generations to come. The Bible tells us that the sins of the fathers will be carried to the third and fourth generation. That's why it's important for parents to imitate the humility of Jesus—and break the chain.

I believe I am modeling the life I'd like my children to live as far as sincerely serving the Lord and respecting the roles of authority God has

established. I do let them know I don't do everything right and that God loves me and them still. I also let them know that I access His forgiveness—often—and trust Him to complete the work He's begun in me. I want them to know the realness of God and His involvement in our lives, but I don't ever want to hinder them by my wrong responses or portray hypocrisy.

—DORI, mother of four

More often than not, when our children don't behave the way we want them to—whether it's throwing a fit or not showing proper appreciation in front of relatives—we react, not out of care or concern for their ultimate well-being, but out of fear and pride over our own emotions. What I've learned is that more often than not, the exact things I dislike in my own children's behavior are a reflection of my own actions.

—SAMI, mother of two

As much as I would like to say I am a servant leader, if I am real I will say I am self-serving more than I care to be. I homeschool my girls and I do put their godly education above everything else. Discipleship is a big deal to our family, especially our children, but I am not the most compassionate mom. I often want to say, "Suck it up!" when I see a scratch—and sometimes I do. It is hard for me to stop what I am doing if I am in the middle of something when they need me. I love being their mom and the Lord is purifying my heart.

—PAIGE, mother of three

My husband and I struggle some with leadership in the home. He is on permanent disability and it causes some challenges, especially when he isn't feeling up to taking a lead role. But I think, thanks to the Lord, we are teaching our kids that we love them enough to try to lead them in the right direction.

—JOANNE, mother of two

Pause & Reflect

- What's your first response to difficult news? Do you tend to become defensive or critical of others? What's your first reaction when you fail at something or make a mistake? What does this tell you about how you're doing with humility?

- When has pride prevented you from admitting to yourself and others that you or your child had a behavior problem? How did you Edge God Out? How can you invite God in the next time?

- When was the last time fear or pride led you away from applying corrective discipline or apologizing to your child? How can God help you in this area from now on?

- Think of a time when competition and comparison with other families led you to pride, fear, and poor use of your resources of time and energy. What difference would it have made if you'd sought God's help through prayer in deciding what to do?

- Do you think the members of your family would call you a servant leader or a self-serving leader? Would you agree? Why or why not?

- How do you think the people in your family would describe your leadership in the following situations?

    a time of crisis

    a time of failure

    a time of victory

    a time of plenty

    a time of want

- How would you like to improve in these areas? How could studying the example of Jesus help?

- How could humbly turning to God to help you with your struggles benefit your children, too?

THREE

An Audience of One

PRINCIPLE 3
To Lead Like Jesus, Focus on God—Not Others

> *There's another kind of EGO—Exalt God Only. That's what Jesus did, and what we need to do as parents. Think of all the time and energy we could save if we stopped comparing ourselves and our families to others and focused on what God wants our families to be. As Tricia points out in this chapter, He's the One we're here to please.*

"You should get to know Skyler's wife, Tara," my husband, John, told me one day after he'd spent time with his coworker Skyler. "I think you'd like her."

"I met Tara, remember, at the company Christmas party," I said. "Maybe I'll invite them over sometime."

But deep in my heart I had no plans for getting together. In our ten-minute conversation months before, I'd learned enough about Tara to know I didn't measure up. She was a 4-H mom who grew a huge garden, stamped her own cards, canned her own jellies, and baked pies—from scratch. Her older son was in the "gifted" program at school, had won the county spelling bee, and was a brown belt in karate. Every time she told me about another of her or her family's accomplishments, my heart beat with a *failure, failure, failure* rhythm about my own life.

Months passed. Again John brought up the idea of getting together with Skyler and Tara's family. I kept making excuses—until one day I asked God to show me people in my life to whom I needed to demonstrate His love. Skyler and Tara's names popped into my mind.

Was this a direct answer to my prayer? I assumed it was. I still worried I wouldn't measure up, but I had a feeling this was something God wanted me to do. With reluctance I made the call and invited them over.

"We'd love to come," Tara said. "I'll even bring a homemade peach pie. My freezer is full of them."

I gritted my teeth and told her that would be nice.

To my amazement, when they showed up that Friday we hit it off, talking as if we'd been friends forever. Yes, Tara gardened and baked, but she was caring and thoughtful, too.

That night, John and I invited them to Bible study and church, and they came the following week. Soon they were a regular fixture in our church and our home, and each week it was amazing to see them grow in their relationship with Christ.

It wasn't until months later that I confessed to Tara my intimidation. I was surprised when she laughed. "Really? I was intimidated by *you*," she told me. "You're an author and a homeschooling mom. I didn't think I could compare."

Isn't that how it is? So often we separate ourselves from others by comparing our weaknesses to their strengths and falling short. We focus on ourselves, not on the God who made each of us for His purposes, with talents and gifts and ways in which we can work for Him.

Pause & Reflect

- What was the last time you compared yourself to someone else and came up short?
- How can you move out of your comfort zone and show appreciation for someone else instead?
- Why is it easier to focus on ourselves than on God? If you could see God, would it be easier to put Him first? Why or why not?

WHAT JESUS DID

Concentrating on ourselves and on others' opinions is a far cry from the example of Jesus. If we're to lead our children as He led, we need to focus on His Father as He did.

> Every year Jesus' parents traveled to Jerusalem for the Feast of Passover. When he was twelve years old, they went up as they always did for the Feast. When it was over and they left for home, the child Jesus stayed behind in Jerusalem, but his parents didn't know it. Thinking he was somewhere in the company of pilgrims, they journeyed for a whole day and then began looking for him among relatives and neighbors. When they didn't find him, they went back to Jerusalem looking for him.
>
> The next day they found him in the Temple seated among the teachers, listening to them and asking questions. The teachers were all quite taken with him, impressed with the sharpness of his answers. But his parents were not impressed; they were upset and hurt.
>
> His mother said, "Young man, why have you done this to us? Your father and I have been half out of our minds looking for you."
>
> He said, "Why were you looking for me? Didn't you know that I had to be here, dealing with the things of my Father?" But they had no idea what he was talking about. (Luke 2:41-50, MSG)

Everything Jesus did was about the other kind of EGO—Exalt God Only. It was an act of worship. According to Dictionary.com, *worship* means "reverent honor and homage paid to God or a sacred personage, or to any object regarded as sacred."

Any time we pay more attention to our own pride or egos, we're worshiping ourselves rather than God. We need to think of ourselves less. Jesus was a perfect example for us. He worshiped God in prayer. He pointed those around Him to God. He followed God's commands.

Even though He *was* God, Jesus didn't lift up His own ego or pride. Instead, He depended on God the Father as His source for everything—including His self-esteem and security:

> *Jesus gave them this answer: "I tell you the truth, the Son can*
> *do nothing by himself; he can do only what he sees his Father*
> *doing, because whatever the Father does the Son also does.*
> *For the Father loves the Son and shows him all he does.*
> *Yes, to your amazement he will show him even greater things*
> *than these. . . . By myself I can do nothing; I judge only as I*
> *hear, and my judgment is just, for I seek not to please myself*
> *but him who sent me." (John 5:19-20, 30)*

Think about that! Jesus was Lord, yet He looked to the Father and depended on Him in everyday matters. Jesus not only worshiped the Father with His praise, but with everyday life. Shouldn't I be willing to do the same? Shouldn't each of us parents be willing to bring everything before God and say, "I can't do anything myself. I only do what God asks me to do. I depend on Him for everything"?

I often think like this during my morning quiet time, after I've read God's Word and prayed. When His awesomeness is fresh on my mind, I know I'd be foolish to do anything else.

But then, through the day, things change. I don't know about you, but sometimes God is the last person I think about when I get in over my head or when I'm making a decision, big or small. I'm prone to think about myself and looking good to others. I consider:

- What will my neighbor think?
- Will the other moms think I'm a bad mom if I don't [fill in the blank]?
- Will I be the only person at church not volunteering?
- Will my kids feel bad if they don't have what everyone else does?

As you can tell from these questions, when I'm worried about what others think it's because I'm concerned about how I look. I'm afraid I won't measure up. I'm worried about myself more than about what God wants me to do—or who He wants me to be.

I can't tell you how many activities I've signed my kids up for or how many events I've participated in because I wanted to look good—and wanted my kids to look good—to other people. My calendar became crammed and our family life suffered. And, of course, I took my eyes off God.

I'm terrible about comparing myself to other parents. I'm getting better, but I often feel like everyone else is doing a better job raising their kids than I am. I take the kids' faults personally, for the most part. Jesus is the only place I can turn. He often reminds me that I can only do this with His help and that if I trust Him and His ways, the kids will likely turn out fine.

—JOANNE, mother of two

The only parent I've ever compared myself to is my dad—and even then, not from a competitive standpoint. It's more a case of, am I providing my son and daughter with the skills and character my dad encouraged in me? I think it would be pointless for me to compare myself to another parent, because I would always be looking over my shoulder. Which is a lousy way to live.

—BRETT, father of two

ALTARING YOUR EGO

The mirror image of Edging God Out is Exalting God Only, and the only way to make the transformation is to do some altaring. *Altaring* is not misspelled. That's exactly what we have to do—put our egos on the altar.

If you didn't grow up in church, this idea of "putting something on the altar" may be unfamiliar. The altar is in the front of the church, the area before the platform where the minister preaches. Going to the altar usually means bringing yourself before God and other witnesses to share a need or request with Him or to make a commitment to Him. For example, a preacher might speak about how parents should be gentle with their children. If you realize you've been harsh with yours, and want to change, you might decide to step up to the altar after the sermon to pray. It's a way to deal with the matter before walking out the door, a time to put yourself and your issues before God—while the matter is fresh in your mind.

I struggle with my weight, and for the longest time I wondered if I would be accepted by other moms and women since I am a plus-size gal. So often it seems as if I live in Barbie Town and Country, where every mom seems to be . . . a size 6 or less. A few months ago I turned this over to God. I admitted failures and how I had made poor choices that got me to the point I was physically, emotionally, spiritually, and mentally drained. I told God that I would honor Him by making better choices. I realized I could choose to be confident or I could choose to not be. Confidence was entirely up to me in any situation. God had already given me a spirit—not of fear and timidity—but of love, power, and self-discipline.

—WENDY, mother of four

The altar is a place of sacrifice. This symbolism goes back to a time when Old Testament priests would sacrifice animals on a physical altar to cover the Israelites' sin. The animals sacrificed were those provided by the people who, instead of keeping the animals for their own use, turned them over to God.

Putting our egos on the altar means to consider things in our lives that Edge God Out—our self-absorption, pride, and self-sufficiency—and bring them before God. We don't need to do this in front of an Old Testament altar. We don't even need to do this at the altar of a church (though we can). Anytime and anywhere we can take the spotlight off ourselves, get away to a quiet place, and exalt God—which means giving Him His rightful place in our life.

Whether we need to do this weekly, daily, or hourly, eventually we'll see—as Jesus did—that God is most important. The more we do this, giving our whole selves to God, the more worship becomes a way of life—and the goal of leading our families.

Here's a diagram that shows how we can "altar our egos" and Exalt God Only:

EXALTING GOD ONLY

As the object of my worship
As the source of my security and self-worth
As the omniscient audience and Judge of my life decisions

Humility
- Something lived but never claimed
- Looking out the window rather than in the mirror to praise
- A kingdom perspective of cause and effect

Confidence
- Resting assured in God's nature, goodness, purpose, plan, process, and provision
- Transparency and effectiveness
- Proceeding in faith one step at a time

Community and Fellowship
Contentment and Generosity
Trust and Truth
Inspiration and Commitment

How to Altar My Leadership EGO

- Embrace an eternal perspective of the *here and now* in light of the *then and there*
- Seek to lead for a higher purpose
  Beyond success
  Beyond significance
  To obedience and surrendered service
- Scrupulously assess my level of trust and surrender to what I believe about God, His kingdom, and His claim on my life and leadership
- Seek the promised guidance of the Holy Spirit, the ultimate coach

PUTTING GOD FIRST IN YOUR PARENTING

As Phil explained in the previous chapter, leading like Jesus means leading your family with humility—avoiding the pride and fear that cause us to Edge God Out. Humility is an attitude that reflects a keen understanding of our limitations. *People with humility don't think less of themselves; they just think of themselves less.* That grows out of having confidence in God.

When we replace our tendency to Edge God Out with Exalting God Only, we influence our kids in a way that points them to Christ. Even after we're gone, our influence will be seen in the ones God has entrusted to our care. A bit of us will live on—not only in the looks of our children, but in their behavior, too.

But how does Exalting God Only look in the everyday rush of parenting? I found out during a very busy time of my life.

My calendar was in chaos. I was having trouble making wise choices about my commitments and my family's activities. One night I broke down crying from being overwhelmed.

My husband, John, asked if we could sit down and go over my schedule. He wanted us to look at everything I'd committed to and figure out where the problem was. He started by asking me to make a list of everything I did in a week.

I scoffed. "You don't have enough paper," I said. Feeling a burden heavy on my shoulders, I started going through the list—caring for our home and children, my work projects, my volunteering, my church service, and all the kids' activities.

After everything was listed, John helped me to rate everything on a scale of one through four. The "ones" were things I *had* to do, such as feeding the kids and homeschooling. The "twos" were things I *should* do, like laundry and housecleaning. The "threes" were things I enjoyed doing and that helped me, such as Bible study and exercise class. The "fours," I discovered, were things I did because I was afraid to say no, or because I wanted to look good or have my kids look good.

To refocus and get a better handle on my schedule, I cut out all the fours. I even cut out some threes, realizing that even though they were good things, it wasn't the right season for them.

Evaluating my activities helped my schedule, and it gave me a glimpse into my heart. I was trying to get others—even God—to love me because of things I did. I realized, though, that God loves me already. When I focus on Him and His plans for me, I can find peace—and have confidence in the things I choose, knowing I'm doing them for God alone.

Unfortunately, right now in my life, I find that I tend to Edge God Out. I have to actually schedule quiet time to get Bible study or devotion time in. As a wife, mother, full-time employee, and graduate school student, most days I get to the end of the day and find that I was not diligent in keeping to my quiet time schedule. I start devotional series, book studies, and the like, but end up dropping them halfway through. I find that if I schedule my quiet time into my calendar, it helps me keep that quiet time.

—BETSY, mother of three

In my work I have definitely taken a pleasing-others approach over a pleasing-God model. Early in my career I was more consumed with progressing through the career ladder and being promoted at work and achieving all I could professionally. Oftentimes this meant late nights at work and missed family activities which led to strife between my wife and me. In recent years that has definitely improved but it seems to be a constant battle, especially as I progress in my level of responsibility at work. I tell my kids constantly, we have to make decisions every day that make people around us see Jesus in us without ever saying His name or preaching to them. In other words, [our actions do] the talking. But that's not always easy, as my kids have seen.

—TOMMY, father of two

I think I am improving on this people-pleasing issue. I was a teen mom when I had my daughter. I wanted nothing more than to please other women, to gain their approval of how I was caring for my baby. It was heartbreaking for me when I was judged for my sin rather than how I was taking care of her. This area of people-pleasing spilled over into all areas of my life. It wasn't until God showed me that my life is for an audience of One that I [realized I] needed to please Him only. Sometimes it still gets the best of me.

—HEATHER, mother of three

Looking at my family's schedule, we don't have a lot of free time—but a lot of church-related activities fill our days. My wife and I were just talking about this subject a couple of weeks ago. It seems we are always so busy, but we are doing good things centered around God's work. My biggest fear is that we get so busy in our lives that we begin to Edge God Out even though our lives are mostly centered on His work. I often wonder if we are getting "fed" ourselves, because we are so busy serving and teaching others that we neglect our own family's growth.

—TOMMY, father of two

THE ONE WHO MATTERS

True worship requires that my eyes are on God, not on others. He is the audience of One that I live my life for.

Jesus was scathing in His judgment of the scribes and Pharisees, whom He called hypocrites because they did their good deeds to be seen by men:

> **Everything they do is done for men to see: . . . they love the
> place of honor at banquets and the most important seats
> in the synagogues; they love to be greeted in the marketplaces
> and to have men call them "Rabbi." (Matthew 23:5-7)**

I hate to think of all the "good" things I've done for the same reason. And the truth is, God knew the truth! He knew when I did things—like help in the church kitchen—because I wanted to look good. Or when I didn't do things—like inviting Skyler and Tara over for dinner—because I didn't want to look bad in comparison. He knew when I was focused horizontally on others instead of turning my heart vertically toward God.

Two problems result from thinking horizontally. The first is that others' opinions, not God's, become the source of our security and self-worth. The second is that our kids pick up on it. My children have seen firsthand how I've run around cleaning the house for company. They've seen me buy a new outfit for a meeting or, worse, when I've tried to mold *them* into something they're not—in order to make me look good.

Too many of us tell our children, "Don't worry about what the other kids think," then trade in our car for a nicer one with payments we can't really afford. Since our kids follow what we do, we shouldn't be surprised when they succumb to peer pressure.

We don't have to let things continue down this path. Instead of making decisions because of peer pressure—or in order to look good—we need to have our kids join us in loving and serving others "as if you were serving the Lord, not men" (Ephesians 6:7). Worship isn't just about singing praises on Sundays; it's about living lives that glorify God every day of the week.

In our family, the moment my husband, my kids, and I began to "genuinely worship" was when we started serving weekly in children's church. John and I began with just three others, acting out the Bible and application lessons. As our own children grew, they started acting out parts, too. As the years passed, Cory, Leslie, and Nathan led the other kids in praise songs and helped with the sound and lights. Every week we served as a family, and our hearts were full of Jesus. We praised Him with our mouths as we sang favorite Bible songs and praised Him with our bodies the rest of the time.

An amazing thing happened. Soon our kids began serving in other areas, too. They volunteered at vacation Bible school, in youth group, and on mission trips, and performed in front of the church. They were doing "good" things, but not because they wanted to *look* good. Rather, they wanted to glorify and point others to God.

As someone who'd done things the wrong way for so many years, I knew the difference. My soul *felt* the difference.

When you focus on God instead of on yourself or others, your family leadership changes—and so does your family.

Pause & Reflect

- In what areas of parenting—providing, showing love, disciplining, nurturing, spiritual training—do you have the least trouble being humble and God-confident?
- In what areas do you struggle most, wondering who you are and what you're about?
- Are you currently volunteering because you didn't want to say no, or signed your kids up for an activity because "everyone else" did? How would it feel if you didn't have those things on your calendar?
- How might you be giving your kids the idea that pleasing others (horizontal) is more important than pleasing God (vertical)? What steps can you take to change that?
- Imagine giving yourself a blank calendar as a gift. Tell yourself to only fill in the activities you believe God is calling you to—the things that benefit your family most. What things would be there? What things would you leave off? Now go out, buy that calendar, and start fresh!

Points to Ponder about the *Heart* of Leading Like Jesus as a Parent

- The focus of the heart is on loving God—and realizing that when all is said and done, what's really important is who you love and who loves you.

- As you consider the heart issues of parenting, a primary question you have to ask yourself is, "Am I a servant leader or a self-serving leader?"

- The heart of a self-serving parent Edges God Out by putting something in God's place, trusting something other than God, and valuing other opinions above God's.

- Edging God Out results in two kinds of EGO problems—false pride and fear, which cause separation, comparison, and distortion of the truth.

- The mirror image of Edging God Out is Exalting God Only, which requires "altaring" your leadership EGO.

- To parent like Jesus, you must worship God only, depend on God completely, and exalt God as your only audience, authority, and Judge.

- When you "altar" your parenting EGO and Exalt God Only, false pride and fear are replaced by humility and God-grounded confidence.

PART II

THE HEAD

The journey to leading like Jesus as a parent starts in the *heart*, with your motives and intent. Those motives and intent then travel through the *head*, where you store your beliefs about parenting.

Jesus proclaimed that leadership—in your case, parenting—is first an act of service. He spent three years teaching this point of view to His disciples. Some people think servant leadership means you're trying to please everyone. Yet that's not what Jesus meant. Did He try to please everyone? When He washed the feet of the disciples and sent them out as His ambassadors, was He commissioning them to do whatever the people wanted?

The answer to both questions is no. Jesus was completely focused on pleasing His Father as His audience of One. He sent His disciples to help people understand the good news and to live according to the values of God's kingdom, not to do whatever they wanted.

In this section, Ken explains the importance of *vision and direction*—the leadership side of being a servant-leader parent. Tricia emphasizes values, an important part of servant leadership. Phil ends Part II with encouragement to stay focused on the primary *purpose* of your family.

FOUR

Family Values

PRINCIPLE 4

To Lead Like Jesus, Discover Your Family's Mission and Take It On

One of your many responsibilities as a parent is to guide your family. Drawing from the teachings of the Bible, Ken explains why establishing vision and direction is vitally important—and shows how to get your family headed on the right path.

In the 1980s I coauthored a book with Spencer Johnson. *The One Minute Manager* spent two years on *The New York Times* bestseller list and became very well known. This little book taught the power of clear goal setting, catching people doing things right, and reprimanding or redirecting efforts when they're off base.

Naturally, the success of that book had a major influence on my family. My son, Scott, who's a great speaker, loves to start his sessions by saying, "Everybody wants to know what it was like to be the One Minute Son." People always laugh.

But then Scott continues, "When I was young I got in trouble a lot. I always hoped I would get punished like my friends—sent to my room or even spanked. But no, I had to go down to the dinner table and talk to my mother, father, and sister about how my behavior was inconsistent with the family values—which, of course, we had established at an off-site retreat."

While Scott says that in a kidding way, the truth is that Margie and I were very clear with our kids about the vision and direction of our family. If you ask Scott, he'll be quick to recall some of those dinner sessions. They usually began with me saying something like, "Well, Scott, you've done it again. Setting off those firecrackers with your friend could have started a fire. Tell me, how does that fit in with our family vision?"

Vision is important because leadership is about going somewhere. If your family members don't know where you're trying to take them, they'll have a hard time getting there—let alone getting excited about the journey. You need a compelling family vision, too.

When it comes to discovering that vision, there are four parts:

Purpose: What business is your family in?

Picture of the Future: What will your family's future look like if you are accomplishing your purpose?

Values: What does your family stand for?

Goals: What needs to be accomplished?

A compelling vision tells you who you are (purpose), where you're going (your picture of the future), and what will guide your journey (your values). Once your vision is established, you can create goals to inform family members about what they need to focus on right now. A compelling vision gives goals real meaning.

Later in the chapter you'll discover how to find your family's vision. For now, let me open the doors to our living room and share the vision that Scott wasn't living up to.

OUR FAMILY'S VISION

So what did our family stand for? First, when it came to our family's *purpose*, we were in the quality of life and service business. We wanted to make sure we had access to the basics of life: food, shelter, money, love, and support. At the same time we wanted to foster servant hearts in our family—hearts committed to serving and nurturing others.

Second, our *picture of the future* was that all members of our family would become loving, caring people who were good citizens in the community and the world. To us, good citizenship meant being willing to generously share our time, talent, and treasure for the benefit of others.

Third, our *values* were integrity, relationships, success, and teamwork. We set goals for Scott and Debbie around these four values. We also made sure these weren't just words. To the best of our ability, Margie and I explained what these words looked like in ways our children could understand.

As to the first value—integrity—I told our kids what my dad always told me: "When all is said and done, the one thing you want to hold true to in life is your integrity. Can people count on your word? Do you not only tell the truth, but when you make a commitment, do you keep it?"

Truth-telling is important to us. Our kids were familiar with the fictional story about young George Washington and the cherry tree. Do you remember the story? It goes something like this:

George Washington's father came to him one day and asked, "George, did you cut down the cherry tree?"

Young George's alleged reply was, "Father, I cannot tell a lie. I did."

Rather than punishing him, George's father praised him for telling the truth.

Scott, who was always a jokester, came to me one day. "Dad, I have a little twist on the George Washington fable." And he proceeded to tell me the following story:

One day a father came to his son. "Son, did you knock over the outhouse?"

"No, Father, I didn't," the son said.

The father told him the George Washington story and then asked his son again, "Did you knock down the outhouse?"

This time the son said, "Father, I cannot tell a lie. I did."

With that, his father bopped him on the side of the head.

The boy, a little confused, looked up at his father. "Father, I'm puzzled. You told me that when George Washington was honest about cutting down the cherry tree, his father praised and rewarded him for telling the truth. But when I told you that I pushed over the outhouse, you hit me."

His father looked at him and frowned. "Son, one difference in the story. George Washington's father was not *in* the cherry tree."

Although it isn't in our top four rank-ordered values, humor is also very important to our family!

As to the second value—relationships—we wanted our kids to have loving, supporting friendships. When they interacted with their friends, we didn't permit bullying, teasing, or picking on each other.

Our family strives to show honor, be kind, serve others, and be respectful. We don't always get it right. Sometimes we don't even come close, but we are always growing and learning as we go.

—MICHELLE, mother of five

When it comes to parenting, I want my kids to know that our relationship with God colors every choice we make. They know we don't have much money to spend on clothes, but we spend a lot of money supporting missionaries. They know we pray and seek God's leadership for all decisions. They see Bibles all over the house, and they know God's Word influences everything we do. They know when things are hard, we look to God for joy and peace. They hear us talking about God as a natural part of our daily conversations. We seek to love God with all we've got—heart, mind, soul, and strength.

—CHRISTY, mother of two

We also wanted them to respect adults. We taught Scott and Debbie that when grownups came to the house, our kids should greet them, shake their hands, and if we weren't home, offer them something to drink and sit and talk with them until we got home.

As to the third value—success—we focused on academic achievement. We felt our children needed to go to college, so they would have better opportunities for success as adults. We set goals for their education and monitored their progress.

Because learning was so integral to our family's success value, we encouraged Scott and Debbie to get into activities that required them to learn new skills. At ten, Debbie got interested in horseback riding. She learned how to take care of her horse, Chelsea, as well as how to ride her in competitive events. Scott became an avid skier and competed in downhill events.

Their learning continued after we started Blanchard Training and Development in 1979. It really was a family business. We taught Scott and Debbie how to score leadership instruments, package materials that needed to be shipped, and do other tasks to help our small staff. In the process, they learned some of the concepts we were teaching. For example, we told them that if they were praised for something they truly valued or had been working on, they should acknowledge the person who praised them by saying, "Thank you so much for that praise/compliment. I appreciate your noticing, because that's important to me." When they would say that, our friends were quite impressed. They'd say, "Your kids are really something."

When it came to our family's fourth value—teamwork—everyone had chores around the house. When we first moved to California, Debbie was nine and Scott was eleven. Every Saturday morning was family chores time. We believed we were all part of running our house, and everybody had specific responsibilities. One thing we *didn't* get on our kids' backs about was how clean their rooms were. Margie and I tend to be messy ourselves, so we didn't feel we could be too critical in that department. But we did establish a rule that if Amelia, who helped us with housekeeping, was going to clean up the kids' rooms, she at least had to be able to get through the door!

Margie and I realized that if we didn't provide our family with a clear vision to serve, our kids would end up serving only themselves. They'd become self-centered. We wanted to get into their hearts that life was not just about them. As the Bible says:

> *Where there is no vision, the people are*
> *unrestrained. (Proverbs 29:18, NASB)*

Pause & Reflect

- **What does your family stand for?**
- **Our family's values are *integrity, relationships, success,* and *teamwork*. If you had to choose four words to describe your family's values, what would they be?**

THE VISION OF JESUS

Jesus was clear about His own reasons for coming to this planet, and clearly stated them. Here are just two examples:

"Don't think I've come to make life cozy. I've come to cut—make a sharp knife-cut between son and father, daughter and mother, bride and mother-in-law—cut through these cozy domestic arrangements and free you for God." (Matthew 10:34-35, MSG)

When Jesus was eating supper at Matthew's house with his close followers, a lot of disreputable characters came and joined them. When the Pharisees saw him keeping this kind of company, they had a fit, and lit into Jesus' followers. "What kind of example is this from your Teacher, acting cozy with crooks and riffraff?"

Jesus, overhearing, shot back, "Who needs a doctor: the healthy or the sick? Go figure out what this Scripture means: 'I'm after mercy, not religion.' I'm here to invite outsiders, not coddle insiders." (Matthew 9:10-13, MSG)

And right from the beginning, Jesus expressed a clear purpose and mission for His disciples. He called them not just to become fishermen, but to a greater purpose:

> Walking along the beach of Lake Galilee, Jesus saw two brothers: Simon (later called Peter) and Andrew. They were fishing, throwing their nets into the lake. It was their regular work. Jesus said to them, "Come with me. I'll make a new kind of fisherman out of you. I'll show you how to catch men and women instead of perch and bass." They didn't ask questions, but simply dropped their nets and followed. (Matthew 4:18-20, MSG)

It's one thing to have a self-centered focus—fishing. It's another to take that focus and redirect it to God's purposes—being fishers of men.

An effective mission statement for your family should express a higher purpose for the greater good that gives meaning to the efforts of each family member. If each person doesn't understand your purpose as a family or isn't excited and passionate about it, your family as a unit will begin to lose its way.

JESUS PICTURES THE FUTURE

Jesus outlined a clear picture of the future for His disciples when He gave them the following charge:

> "God authorized and commanded me to commission you: Go out and train everyone you meet, far and near, in this way of life, marking them by baptism in the threefold name: Father, Son, and Holy Spirit. Then instruct them in the practice of all I have commanded you. I'll be with you as you do this, day after day after day, right up to the end of the age." (Matthew 28:18-20, MSG)

Your picture of the future answers the question, "What will the future look like if things are running as planned?"

As you view your family's future, it's important to distinguish between *goals* and *picture of the future*. A goal is a specific event that, once achieved, becomes a piece of history to be superseded by a new goal. A picture of the future is an ongoing, evolving, hopeful look into the future that stirs the hearts and minds of family members who know they will never see its end or its limit.

If things are running as planned, my children will have a heart for ministry and a passion for sharing their authentic relationship with God.

—WENDY, mother of four

THE VALUES OF JESUS

When the Pharisees sought to test Jesus with a question—"Teacher, what is the greatest commandment in the law?"—Jesus was clear about the values that should guide our journey:

> Jesus said, "'Love the Lord your God with all your passion and prayer and intelligence.' This is the most important, the first on any list. But there is a second to set alongside it: 'Love others as well as you love yourself.' These two commands are pegs; everything in God's Law and the Prophets hangs from them." (Matthew 22:37-40, MSG)

He also proclaimed the upside-down values of His kingdom:

> "You're blessed when you've lost it all.
> God's kingdom is there for the finding.

You're blessed when you're ravenously hungry.

Then you're ready for the Messianic meal.

You're blessed when the tears flow freely.

Joy comes with the morning.

"Count yourself blessed every time someone cuts you down or throws you out, every time someone smears or blackens your name to discredit me. What it means is that the truth is too close for comfort and that that person is uncomfortable. You can be glad when that happens— skip like a lamb, if you like!—for even though they don't like it, I do . . . and all heaven applauds. And know that you are in good company; my preachers and witnesses have always been treated like this." (Luke 6:20-23, MSG)

Your values will frame the behavior of your family members as they turn your family's purpose and picture of the future into reality.

THE GOALS OF JESUS

Throughout Jesus' ministry, He was clear with His disciples on direction and goals. For example, when He sent out the Twelve on the first commission, He gave them the following instructions:

> *"Do not go among the Gentiles or enter any town of the*
> *Samaritans. Go rather to the lost sheep of Israel.*
> *As you go, preach this message: 'The kingdom of heaven*
> *is near.' Heal the sick, raise the dead, cleanse those*
> *who have leprosy, drive out demons. Freely you have*
> *received, freely give." (Matthew 10:5-8)*

When you set goals in your family, it will help members determine what they should focus on right now.

PARENTS AS VISION CASTERS

What's the purpose of your family? What's your picture of the future? What values will guide your journey? What goals do you want family members to focus on today?

If you can't answer those questions, you don't have a compelling vision. Without clear vision and direction, the rest of your parenting skills and effort won't matter. You can't be a servant leader if there's nothing to serve.

If you cut children loose without any direction or guidelines, they'll lose their way. The family unit will be fractured as everyone heads off in the direction that he or she decides is best. Guidelines are boundaries that channel energy in a certain direction. It's like a river. If you take away the banks, it won't be a river anymore; it will be a large puddle, devoid of momentum and direction. What keeps the river flowing are its banks, its boundaries.

In companies, people look to the leader for vision and direction. In families, that role falls to the parents. As the diagram below suggests, while you might

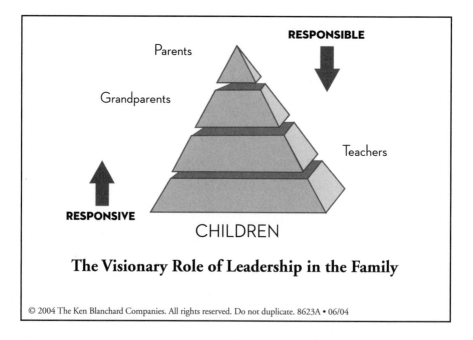

The Visionary Role of Leadership in the Family

involve your children in this process as they get older, the ultimate responsibility for establishing vision and direction remains with you and can't be delegated to others.

Once vision and direction are set, children are expected to be responsive—that is, to live according to your guidelines.

Again, you can't be a servant leader if you don't take care of the leadership part. Don't be afraid of this role. It's not about being bossy; it's about setting up your family to win.

Communication is always the key. We always sit down and have family meetings to address our goals, visions, problems, and situations. Our kids are a big part of our family. We teach them that they have to contribute and work hard with us. If having a new vision includes money management or change of family routine, they are a part of it. For example, instead of going out for dinner or lunch, we cook together at home and have fun. It helps them to feel important and to understand that in life things don't come with pixie dust. They need to work hard to achieve something.

—FERNANDA, mother of two

Our family's vision is for my husband and me to grow more in Christian love for each other and intentionally lead our children according to His love and grace. We also highly encourage each other to serve Jesus in every part of our lives. My husband encourages me to keep walking forward in that. He's a writer and has a gift of encouragement. As parents, we desire to cultivate our children's gifts early and allow them to discover what they are and how they can use that to serve and impact lives around them.

—KENNISHA, mother of three

Pause & Reflect

- Have you ever cast a vision for your family? If so, are you living according to that vision? If not, what do you want your family's vision to be?
- What's your family's purpose? In other words, what business is your family in?
- What's your family's picture of the future? What will it look like if you're accomplishing your purpose?
- What are your family's values? What does your family stand for?
- What are your family's goals? What needs to be accomplished?

FIVE

To Do or Not to Do

PRINCIPLE 5

To Lead Like Jesus, Say Yes to the Best and No to the Rest

> *In a world where to-do lists are long and time always seems too short, setting priorities for a family can be a daunting task. Jesus advised His listeners to make God their top priority: "But seek first his kingdom and his righteousness, and all these things will be given to you as well" (Matthew 6:33). In this chapter, Tricia shows how that can bring your values and goals to life—bringing true riches to your family.*

The first time my pastor asked if I'd be interested in volunteering to help start a Pregnancy Care Center, my mental answer was an immediate *That's nice, but no thank you.* As a homeschooling mom and part-time writer, I had a full plate. I didn't want to be running every which way. I wanted time to spend with my husband and children. We were also already involved as a family in serving on Sundays.

But I told my pastor the politically correct answer, forcing my lips into a smile. "Pastor Daniel," I said, "I'll have to pray about that."

Next morning, as I sat down with my Bible and journal, I was reminded of my promise to pray. To be truthful, my prayer went something like this: "Dear Lord, I know Pastor Daniel means well. I know there is a huge need for help for women facing crisis pregnancies, but my plate is already full. I'm thankful that

I'm able to be home with my kids. I'm thankful that I get to write. I would like to help, Lord, but doesn't he see I'm helping others instead? My words are going out all over the world, sharing Your good news. Help me find a good way to tell Pastor Daniel no."

As I sat there I felt a stirring within, and I was sure it was the Holy Spirit trying to get my attention. *What are you doing to help people in your own community?* I knew the thought wasn't from me. Could this be God speaking?

Wouldn't it be nice to give others the same type of help you received? the inner voice said.

That last thought especially struck a chord. I recalled how, years before when I was a pregnant teenager, my mother and grandmother's Bible study group had supported me. Because of their love, I'd considered giving my bruised and battered heart to Jesus. They hadn't turned their backs on me even though I'd messed up big time—which made me think that maybe God hadn't turned His back on me, either. One day, when I was six months pregnant, I turned my life over to Him.

Sitting on my couch all those years later, Bible in hand, I knew that God was trying to tell me something. He wanted me to get involved.

Soon I started working with the pastor and two other women to get the center up and running. More volunteers joined our ranks.

I never expected God to work so quickly. Within a year we had a donated building. The abortion rate in our county was down by one third, and many young men and women were coming to know Christ through the love shown to them by dedicated volunteers.

I also never expected my husband and children to get so involved. They were there on evenings and weekends, helping to fix up the Victorian house we'd been given to use for the center. My daughter babysat for our teen mother support groups. We celebrated as I shared stories of the wonderful things happening in the pregnancy center. We enjoyed inviting young mommies and couples into our home for meals and mentoring.

I'd believed I didn't have time for service. But following God's direction not only changed our community, it also helped my family to determine our values and choices.

We became a service-oriented family. What I thought would take me away from my husband and kids actually pulled us together. It also set a foundation for our other core values and guided our future priorities.

Once your children understand the vision for your family and have a picture of where you want to take them—and why—the next step is to model what you believe. By living each day according to your family's values and accomplishing the established goals, you set a good example that shows your kids what it means to live the family's vision. In essence, you lead by becoming a servant of that vision.

THE PRIORITIES OF JESUS

Jesus set priorities for Himself, for His disciples, and for us—many of them nonnegotiable. As noted in the previous chapter, for instance, He rank-ordered two values:

1. Love God with all your heart, soul, and mind.

2. Love your neighbor as yourself.

But rank-ordered values alone won't accomplish your family's purpose or turn your picture of the future into reality. You need to translate those values into behaviors. That's what Jesus did throughout His three-year public ministry. Here's just one case in point:

> Later Jesus was going about his business in Galilee. He didn't want to travel in Judea because the Jews there were looking for a chance to kill him. It was near the time of Tabernacles, a feast observed annually by the Jews.
>
> His brothers said, "Why don't you leave here and go up to the Feast so your disciples can get a good look at the works you do? No one who intends to be publicly known does everything behind the scenes. If you're

serious about what you're doing, come out in the open and show the world." His brothers were pushing him like this because they didn't believe in him either.

Jesus came back at them, "Don't crowd me. This isn't my time. It's your time—it's *always* your time; you have nothing to lose. The world has nothing against you, but it's up in arms against me. It's against me because I expose the evil behind its pretensions. You go ahead, go up to the Feast. Don't wait for me. I'm not ready. It's not the right time for me." (John 7:1-8, MSG)

Jesus filled His schedule and picked His battles according to His priorities—choosing on one day to heal, on another to teach, on another to spend time alone with His Father. Doing the same in your family will show your kids how to live out your family values, allow them to be accountable, and help you measure their progress.

True success in servant leadership depends on how clearly the values are defined, ordered, and lived by the leader.

YOUR FAMILY VALUES

Every family needs three or four core values to stand on—and to set priorities. Why only three or four? If you really want to affect behavior, you can't emphasize more because people can't focus on that many.

Pause & Reflect

- If someone who didn't know you asked what your family's values are, what would you say?
- If that person asked how you live out those values as a family, what could you point to as evidence?

When I think about our family, the core values that come to mind are *service, compassion,* and *evangelism.* Those words summarize our work in the pregnancy center, in children's church, and even in my writing and my husband's current ministry job.

When I asked my 19-year-old daughter what three words she thought summarized our core values, she chose *service, transparency,* and *hospitality.* This made me smile; even though we used different words, they reflected the same idea. The values were part of us. As a family we love to serve others, open our hearts, share our lives, and share our faith.

The activities we get involved in reflect our belief that our family isn't just on earth to make ourselves comfortable, but to reach out to others in need. Without realizing it, John and I put a focus on these values not only by our words but also with our behaviors.

A wise man noted that it was only in the past century that the word *priority* went plural. Jesus had one priority: *glorify God.* When we apply His priority to our lives and families, it gives an added level of purpose to our decisions. For example, we might say, "In our family we seek to glorify God by living out our values of service, transparency, and hospitality."

Often we learn what our values are when we follow God and heed His direction for our lives—not before. We discover them as we dedicate our time and resources to Him. The process works like this:

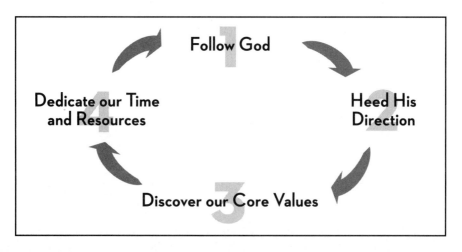

Follow God

Heed His Direction

Discover our Core Values

Dedicate our Time and Resources

We have values as a family but we'd never verbalized them. I finally landed on three values that I think are most important to our family:

1. Growth—[we grow] in our relationship with God, individually and as a family. We are able to encourage each other in our growth so that this core value remains a top priority. Our son is almost twenty-one months old, and we know it's never too early for him to hear the gospel! We do simple Bible studies with him and pray as a family every night.

2. Family Enjoyment—It's important to us to spend time together as a family. Meal times, Bible studies, and recreation times are all perfect examples of moments we want to share with each other daily. To make enough time for this to happen on a regular basis, we have to say no to other things that could take our time. We don't watch much TV, we don't overcommit to work or church activities, and we limit our social lives. Contrary to popular belief, you can't really have it all. You have to choose what's most important. Our family time is sacred to us, so we make decisions accordingly.

3. Service—This core value can be divided into three areas. We serve others in need through our prayers, our finances, and our acts of service. We often find that we are probably far more blessed by serving others than they are by being served!

—JAYNA, mother of one

Our actual core values as a family are [reflected by] going to various local parks and festivals, going to local sporting events, watching LSU and the Saints on TV together, cooking and eating meals together, traveling to visit with close family or having them come stay with us, and going to church together once a week. Again, I am thankful for all of the things we do together and the enjoyment we have in spending these times together, but

I continuously pray for us as a family to grow toward a bond centered on the Lord and not just on each other.

—HAELIE, mother of one

The biggest two core values I have tried to instill into my family are really one and the same. I've always told them to love everyone, because that was Jesus' greatest command to us. I believe the second core value ties right into that—to serve others at every opportunity. We try to look for little things we can do to show that love. One of my little sayings my kids get tired of hearing me say is, "You can lead someone to Jesus without ever saying a word to them. You must live your life showing love and doing little things to show that love they never see anyplace else."

—TOMMY, father of two

TOP PRIORITIES

Life, family, and leadership are all about choices. What do you stand for? How have you chosen family activities to match?

Problems often arise when we try to make our vision line up with our calendar. But it's important to prioritize family values because life is about value conflicts. When these conflicts arise, family members need to know what values they should focus on. Without guidelines, they'll create their own order of priority—which may lead away from fulfilling the purpose and picture of your family's future.

That requires you to manage the family calendar so that *what you do* matches *what you believe.* True success depends on how clearly you define, order, and live your family values.

> *Great family leaders make hard decisions to make sure what they live matches what they believe.*

For many years John and I signed up for things without really giving any mind to how it would affect our marriage, children, or core values. This caused conflict in our family. We weren't leading our children effectively as parents because we didn't understand—or value—who we were together. And we didn't place our focus on what was most important to God.

VERBALIZING VALUES

One of the best ways I know to determine your family's values and priorities is through a fun after-dinner activity. Take some food items from your refrigerator or pantry and read the labels together. Some of the words that describe your favorite foods might be "bold," "organic," "flavorful," "healthy," or "classic." Explain how the words on the label represent what's inside.

Next, use poster board and markers to make a sign—a "label"—for your family. How is your family different from others you know? Let younger kids draw pictures of your family to go with the labels. Then ask, "Do the activities we choose fit and reflect our family's label?" If they don't, discuss what you need to step back from in order to step into what God has designed your family to do.

Once you figure out what needs to be cut out of your lives, consider what activities *would* match what your heart tells you is most important. Write a list of action steps that would lead you to doing what you believe. As you make plans, your family will get a glimpse of who God designed you—as a unit—to be.

Your Family Label

- Name your core values and turn them into a label.
- Determine if your family's activities match your family label.
- Cut out any activities that don't fit your label.
- Figure out what kinds of ministry or service you can do together— ones that match your label.
- Write a list of action steps to accomplish that ministry or service.
- Seek God daily as you strive to live according to His design and serve those He puts into your life.

PICTURING PRIORITIES

An important question for family leaders to ask is, "What do we want to influence?" Parents of a newborn might want to influence when he or she eats or goes to sleep. As the child gets older, the answer usually gets more complicated; you might want to influence the child's manners, schoolwork, respect for elders, responsibilities, and the like.

Once we've identified these areas, we must specify clearly our values and priorities in each—so that parent and child know when the child's behavior is on the right track. What does having good manners mean? When has a child done a good job on homework?

It is hard to model good behavior. Depending on what it is, I struggle with modeling it. But that shows them that I am human, too! Ways I do model good behavior are by loving their daddy, taking them to church, and showing them family is important.

—Regina, mother of two

We try to model good behavior. In fact, our youngest will now call us on things he sees that aren't proper behavior. Our response is to tell him that he is exactly right—we are sorry for not behaving correctly and we ask him to please forgive us. At five, that's a lot easier than it will be in just a few years if the foundation isn't laid properly.

—Allison, mother of three

The key is specifying what carrying out your priorities *looks like*. Just telling a child, "I want you to keep your room clean," is not as helpful as saying, "I want you to keep your room clean. What I mean by a 'clean room' is that your bed is made, your toys and clothes are picked up off the floor, your trash can is emptied, and all your dresser drawers are neat." Even that final statement might need further explanation. While a child might have no trouble understanding what an empty trash can looks like, a "neat" dresser drawer could be more open to debate. For you and the child to know how well the child is doing, "what meeting expectations looks like" has to be clearly specified.

THUMBS UP, THUMBS DOWN

At our house, another way we've helped our children understand the difference between behaviors that do and don't reflect our values and priorities is to play a simple game around the dinner table. It's called the Thumbs-Up/Thumbs-Down Game.

It got started during a six-month period when we opened our home to a young family. The parents, Kayleigh and Nathan, were only teens themselves when they had their children and struggled with leading their young family—so there was a lot of opportunity to teach their kids about values and priorities.

The game is simple. Each person gets a turn to name a behavior; everyone else gives that behavior a thumbs-up or thumbs-down. Here are some examples of behaviors:

- Pushing your brother
- Taking your sister's things without asking
- Listening to and obeying your parents the first time
- Throwing food on the floor
- Offering to help without asking
- Yelling in the house
- Calling each other names
- Offering to share your special treat
- Whining
- Picking up someone else's toys and putting them away

Playing this game gave us a chance to bring up small offenses without a lecture. The kids quickly caught on to what was acceptable and what wasn't.

It also was easy to offer guidance away from the table without saying a word. Many times I praised with a thumbs-up during the day or corrected with a thumbs-down.

Besides reinforcing good behavior, this game made me reconsider what God was calling me to. *Would all the things I spend my time doing get a thumbs-up or thumbs-down from God?* That's a question worth asking, too.

LIVING OUT YOUR VALUES

Leading your family like Jesus isn't just a matter of identifying values and priorities, though. Living them out is what you're aiming for.

I remember the first time I saw one of my kids choose to live out our family values and priorities without my prodding.

My son came home from junior high youth group with a smile on his face. "Mom, our youth leader was looking for a place to have our youth Christmas party. I told him we could have it at our house, because we love having people over."

I smiled and told Cory that would be fine. In the years to come I always made extra food at dinner and bought extra snacks for the weekend because I never knew what additional people we'd have around the dinner table. John and I had told our children many times that we loved opening our home and serving others. But even more than our words, our kids saw it lived out.

Everyone is watching—especially your children. If parents live out their values, kids are ready to follow suit. Jesus lived His values of loving God and loving His neighbors all the way to the cross:

> *"Greater love has no one than this, that he*
> *lay down his life for his friends." (John 15:13)*

When I look back now, I'm thankful that I spent time praying and asking God about whether or not I should volunteer at the Pregnancy Care Center. It's amazing to see that God not only had a plan for me, but also for my children.

He wanted to show me what my husband and I had inside—hearts of service, compassion, and evangelism. He also knew that when we followed Him, our kids would follow us!

Maybe you, too, will discover that the one thing you don't feel you have time for is the very way in which God wants to teach you and your children about becoming servant leaders.

We show God's love to our neighbors. We help them as much as we can. We give food, clothes, emotional support. We have taken almost all of our neighborhood kids to church. Most of them have given their lives to Jesus. We have Bible classes at home and we live a life that reflects Jesus. God's will for us is very important. We don't make one decision without asking Him and praying about it. He is the center of our lives, the Lord of our family. We move as He moves. If He's not moving, we are for sure standing still, knowing that He is God.

—FERNANDA, mother of two

We stand for active faith, for seeing God and His hand in all of our situations and for trusting without worry. As a family, we can reflect these beliefs through our actions, our words, our thoughts, and in what we do with our work and with our free time. We don't always reflect this, though. Why? Sometimes because we are tired, worn out, afraid, or unconfident. But, together as a family, we can stand stronger.

—CAROLINE AND JOEY, parents of two

My family activities don't always show a monument of God's grace. Often it seems that instead of a monument—done and finished and there—I am a visible work under construction, pieced together with glue and duct tape. Often the choices of the moment have me doing schoolwork, housework, other work instead of sitting with my children and speaking words of life into them, sharing with them my favorite verses and telling them how God reached me, rescued me, and reserved me—or about the vision of my life and how that impacts and intersects with theirs. The challenge for me is to utilize the teachable moments and imprint the important lessons and truths upon my children's hearts.

—WENDY, mother of four

Pause & Reflect

- Great family leaders communicate their vision, values, and goals over and over again until family members get them right. What are the vision, values, and goals you are communicating to your family?
- How are you living these out day-to-day?
- You are a monument to the choices you've made. What does the monument you've built say about what you stand for?

SIX

Staying on Course

PRINCIPLE 6

To Lead Like Jesus, Know the Difference Between a Crisis and a Bump in the Road

> *One of the greatest gifts parents can give their children is consistency of purpose. Drawing from the teachings of Jesus, Phil reveals the true purpose of parenting—and shows how to keep your eye on that goal no matter how many distractions everyday family life may send your way.*

When my kids were small, my days were filled with listening to grievances, administering corrective discipline, and reconciling disputes between people who thought their rights had been violated.

And that was my day job!

Because my professional role was to oversee conflict resolution, rarely did others call to tell me they were having a nice day. I got paid to actively listen, be patient, and sort facts from feelings.

The thirty-minute drive home was a rare period of solitude. I was alone with my thoughts. With each mile that passed, the tension of the day trailed behind like the exhaust from my car. My fantasy was that when I walked through the door at home I would be greeted by people who were happy with each other and happy to see me.

This was not always the case. Instead, on the other side of the front door was a whole new set of issues to be addressed.

My son, Phil, now the married father of four lively children, describes the front door experience as leaving "Big World" and entering "Little World." I like that.

When my kids were growing up, the people on the other side of the door—those from Little World—were the dearest in my life. They deserved the best I had to offer, not just leftovers. Listening to grievances, administering discipline, and reconciling disputes happened in this world, too, but at a different level. They involved things like stopped-up toilets, missing homework, skinned knees, and sibling wars. Sometimes it was easy to focus on the problems and miss my purpose as a servant leader: to influence my child's heart.

At work my efforts brought harmony to the company and peace among employees for a season. At home my efforts didn't just matter for that month or year. I knew they wouldn't just affect the lives of my children, but their children, too—as I'm seeing today.

Knowing that was one thing, but making it reality was another. It took figuring out my "would I's," and sticking to them, before I walked through that front door.

Would I afford my family the same level of respect that I gave people at work?

Would I take time to listen before responding?

Would I exhibit patience and perspective, separating accidents from intentional acts?

Standing at the front door, I had a choice: to justify the self-serving attitude of a weary warrior (or a hunter home from the hill) who has earned a quiet moment by the fire, or assume the duties of a servant leader.

Becoming a servant leader is one of the hardest things to do, but the rewards will come. I smile when I see our daughter, LeeAnne, and daughter-in-law, Marion, managing Little World for our seven grandchildren with grace, patience, and servant hearts.

Influencing hearts for generations is the true purpose of our parenting. Thinking of parental roles that way makes it easier to roll up our sleeves, offer respect, exhibit patience, and listen before responding. The truth is, those phrases—

"You act just like your father," or "You sound just like your mother"—can be a good thing!

Purpose is a key part of your family's vision. It describes who you are as a family and clarifies what "business" your family is in. Once your kids know the purpose of your family, your role as a servant-leader parent is to make sure your family's purpose is consistently applied—even when distractions threaten to throw you off course.

SPILLED MILK AND OTHER BUMPS IN THE ROAD

Some days being a servant leader wasn't easy. Some days I made the wrong choice. One thing that helped me with decision-making was realizing the distinction between deliberate and accidental acts.

Don't you hate it when your kids spill their milk? Me, too. There were times I'd get so frustrated. *Don't they know better?*

As a father I had to learn the difference between accidents and misconduct. There are two ways to look at spilled milk. There's the milk spilled because the cup is too large for a young child to handle, or it gets set down wrong or bumped against a plate. Then there's the milk that spills when your child looks you in the eye, cocks an eyebrow, and turns over a cup. Two different actions, two different heart attitudes.

Sometimes we forget this—especially when it concerns something much bigger than milk.

Spilled-Milk Suggestions

- Keep the lines of communication open.
- Never embarrass or frustrate your kids in public.
- Remember the bigger purpose. It's not to make sure the milk never spills. More important is to model servant leadership when the milk *does* spill.

One day, when I was just a teenager, I was driving along a narrow dirt road when a mother with a station wagon full of kids coming the other way drifted into my lane. She must have been distracted. (Who wouldn't be with that many kids in the car?) Attempting to avoid an accident, I turned my car onto the shoulder and hit an embedded rock. The combination of rock, speed, and hillside was enough to flip the car upside down. Within a matter of seconds my feet were hanging over my head. Thankfully I wasn't injured, but the car roof was flattened. And it wasn't my car—it was my dad's.

Eventually the police arrived, and my dad's car was towed to a local garage. The police chief drove me home and informed my dad about the accident. Dad's response was immediate and emotional. Let's just say he went ballistic.

"You will never drive my car again!" was his central theme. Fortunately, the police chief intervened. He suggested my father come down to the garage to look at the car. When Dad saw the damage, he knew how lucky I'd been not to be killed. And when he was assured I was not at fault, his attitude quickly changed.

My dad apologized for overreacting, but the memory stuck. I never wanted to see that reaction again, so I was inclined to cover up accidents and screwups rather than risk my dad's wrath.

Later, when parenting our young children, thinking of my dad's response to the flipped car made me pause in many of my own reactions. It made me ask, "Is this a crisis, or is this a bump in the road?"

I made a conscious effort to respond to accidents like spilled milk—and bigger ones—with as little emotion as possible. Quickly cleaning up an accidental mess, without comment, allows an accident to stay in perspective as a small event. The meal can continue. Accidents are a part of life; they can't be avoided and shouldn't be feared.

A measured response to simple accidents allows heart issues like disrespect or disobedience to stand out. When issues like these are dealt with quickly, with measured consequences, children understand the significance of what they've done. If every unwanted act—willful or not—gets a fiery response, kids never know what's important. If Daddy or Mommy screams just as loud when a TV show is interrupted, what will make young James pause when running into the road when Mom or Dad yells, "Stop!"?

There's a big difference between childishness and foolishness, and I try to discipline appropriately. Dropping or spilling something might be frustrating, but it's just going to crush my child's spirit if I overreact. Willful disobedience, however, can't be overlooked.

—DIANE, mother of two

My parents were always tough on me for both childish and willful behavior, so when I had my daughter, I wanted to be different. There's a fine line between childish behavior and willful, wrong behavior. A childish behavior is the absence of knowledge of something. They are just not aware. We have to be mature enough to recognize and not punish them, but instead, in love, teach them. A willful behavior always has a desire behind it. Is it stress? The need to feel loved? The desire to be the center of attention? Or is it just because they are learning how to deal with personal relationships? All of this has to be taken into consideration and that has to be decided in a split second! Wow! Only the Spirit is able to help us be good parents, understanding not to give the wrong punishment; not to do what our parents did to us.

—FERNANDA, mother of two

PURPOSEFUL RESPONSES TO ON-PURPOSE BEHAVIOR

Most spilled-milk incidents and my car accident were unintentional. But there are times when our children must learn that negative consequences—natural or imposed by parents—should be expected.

My mother taught me an invaluable lesson in consequences when I was three years old. One evening I was sitting in my high chair, eating a bowl of beef stew. I was about three-quarters finished when I decided I wanted to get down and play. My mother asked me if I'd finished my stew.

"Yes," I said.

"All gone?" she asked.

"Yes—all gone!"

Mom looked at me, then at the bowl, which was still partly full. "Are you sure that it is all gone?"

"Yes."

"Well, then—if it's all gone, why don't you turn the bowl over on your head?"

I was three years old—and stubborn—so I did.

I can still remember the feeling of warm, brown stew pouring over my head while Mom tried rather unsuccessfully to keep a straight face. In a small but effective way, she showed me she wasn't going to let my rebellion go unanswered. She was a great example of what it meant to stay on purpose while teaching me the consequences of my willful behavior.

There's an old saying that "behavior is controlled by its consequences." In other words, what happens *after* something occurs is more important than what happens *before*. While all good behavior starts with a clear vision and well-defined goals, the biggest shaper of future actions is the response your kids get to the things they do.

There are four responses you can give to your children's behavior:

1. No response

2. Negative response

3. Positive response

4. Redirection

The most popular parental responses to behavior are no response and negative response. They add up to what Ken calls "leave-alone/zap." In this scenario, you don't respond to anything a child does until he or she does something wrong. Then you leap into action and "zap" your child. It's also become known as "seagull management"—when something goes wrong the parent flies in, makes a lot of noise, dumps on everybody, and flies out. What the child learns is to avoid the punisher, the parent.

So how can you react to your kids' behavior in a way that doesn't detour from your overall parenting purpose? Positive responses and redirection are the best routes to take.

SEE THE BIG PICTURE

Every child makes mistakes, and most aren't fatal. When it comes to spilled milk or poured-out stew, we can either focus on the mess—or we can keep the consistency of purpose in our parenting.

Remember, influencing hearts for generations is parenting's true purpose. To do that, we need to grow children with teachable hearts. That can start when you declare that there are no mistakes in your family, only learning opportunities. It will also encourage your children to "'fess up when they mess up," because they know you won't yell at them if every mistake is a learning opportunity. In such a safe haven, kids are more honest about their missteps instead of hiding them.

Of course, not every moment is a teaching moment. Sometimes it's important just to clean up the mess and move on. But we need to have a purposeful partnership with Jesus Christ when it comes to childrearing. When your children leave your house, what will the condition of their hearts be? Full of pride or egotistical self-preservation? Or full of humility, love, and dedication to God and family?

An elderly woman I knew had raised four children. "They were always so well dressed," she said. "They knew to be seen and not heard. They were always quiet and well-behaved, and I received compliments wherever I went." That may have been true. But each of those four children grew up and had out-of-wedlock pregnancies, were divorced numerous times, and had difficulty keeping jobs. Their mother may have taught them how to act nicely in public, but the true purpose of parenting—influencing hearts for generations—seemed to have been lost on her.

Sometimes the parenting routine of getting children fed, dressed, and clean seems to be the only thing that matters. But if that's all that matters in your home, it'll be the only thing that matters when they leave.

Pause & Reflect

- Think of a current conflict involving you and your kids. Ask yourself: Do my children need to learn a lesson here, or do I just need to work on compliance?
- Remember: If you work only to get your children to comply, you'll miss the opportunity to influence their hearts.

THE PURPOSE-DRIVEN SAVIOR

If you wonder what God thinks about ideal leadership, just take a glimpse of Jesus in the Gospels! When He came into the world, He displayed God's love and truth in His living, breathing purpose.

A key insight into that purpose is contained in His prayer for His disciples, recorded in John 17. Here is a sample:

> "Father, it's time.
> Display the bright splendor of your Son
> So the Son in turn may show your bright splendor.
> You put him in charge of everything human
> So he might give real and eternal life to all in his charge.
> And this is the real and eternal life:
> That they know you,
> The one and only true God,
> And Jesus Christ, whom you sent.

I glorified you on earth
By completing down to the last detail
What you assigned me to do.
And now, Father, glorify me with your very own splendor,
The very splendor I had in your presence
Before there was a world." (John 17:1-5, MSG)

In this wonderful prayer of accountability by the ultimate servant leader, we see that Jesus stayed focused on what He was sent to accomplish. He told His Father, "I glorified you on earth by completing down to the last detail what you assigned me to do" (John 17:4). In total obedience and commitment, Jesus stayed on point. He did not seek to take on other tasks or the agenda others hoped He would fulfill. And He encouraged His followers to do the same:

As they continued their travel, Jesus entered a village. A woman by the name of Martha welcomed him and made him feel quite at home. She had a sister, Mary, who sat before the Master, hanging on every word he said. But Martha was pulled away by all she had to do in the kitchen. Later, she stepped in, interrupting them. "Master, don't you care that my sister has abandoned the kitchen to me? Tell her to lend me a hand."

The Master said, "Martha, dear Martha, you're fussing far too much and getting yourself worked up over nothing. One thing only is essential, and Mary has chosen it—it's the main course, and won't be taken from her." (Luke 10:38-42, MSG)

Pause & Reflect

- List three things that are most likely to pull you off course as a parent. When that happens, what effect does it seem to have on the morale of your spouse and children?

When I'm tired—physically, emotionally, or spiritually—I tend to have a shorter fuse and can get bogged down in the details instead of "keeping the main thing the main thing." I can see when my bad mood or irritability affects the rest of my family and it's a shameful thing. Sometimes I feel almost powerless to stop it, but with prayer and a supportive, forgiving family, we are always able to get right back on track. We moms and wives have such power over the atmosphere of our homes. It's humbling, exciting, and a bit terrifying to recognize the role that God has granted to us!

—DIANE, mother of two

Personal health issues tend to pull me off course. I suffer from chronic migraines, about fifteen a month in a bad month. They tend to be barometric and we live in the South—lots of storms. When I'm going through a tough time with my headaches, I can't be the mother, wife, or friend I want to be. My girls have to fend for themselves more and my husband has to pick up the slack. We end up in a holding pattern until I can get better, then we're back on track.

—CAREN, mother of two

The three things that pull me off course are:

Fatigue—overcommitting myself. Wrong priorities—giving in to the "I have to do it all" lie. Super-Mom Syndrome—setting the bar too high, like all the way to perfection. When I get pulled off course, I end up spread too thin, irritable, and exhausted. And guess what? My family is irritable and exhausted, too. When I go off course, I take them with me. I have to say no—not just for me, but for all of us.

—BETH, mother of four

> ## Tips for Staying on Track
>
> - List the things you're doing right.
> - Don't compare; comparative parenting is a trap. It will bring pride or defeat, neither of which is good.
> - Remember, the One to please in your parenting is your heavenly Father. Because of His forgiveness, grace, and mercy, we're able to be the forgiving, graceful, and merciful parents He's called us to be.

WHEN PURPOSE GETS PERSONAL

Influencing hearts for generations describes the purpose of parents in general. But what about you, specifically? What's your individual purpose, the one unique to you?

Before trying to influence your family, you need to be clear about your personal purpose. A family leader's personal purpose guides and aligns the efforts of those who follow; hidden motives and agendas sabotage trust, the key ingredient in any leader-follower relationship.

What is personal purpose? It's your reason for being.

A purpose is different from a goal in that it has no beginning or end. It's the meaning of the journey, not the destination. Purpose is bigger than any achievement. Your personal purpose is your calling—the reason you were created. In the context of family leadership, your personal purpose must include serving others' best interests, or it becomes manipulation and exploitation—the absolute opposite of leading like Jesus.

Why are you here? What business are you in? Few people have a clear sense of their life's purpose. How can you make good decisions about using your parenting time if you don't know what your purpose is?

The following simple process will help you create a good first draft of your life purpose. To begin, list some of your personal characteristics you feel good about. Use nouns or noun phrases, such as these:

- sense of humor
- teaching skills
- creativity
- energy
- mechanical genius
- passion

- people skills
- patience
- enthusiasm
- communication skills
- happiness
- insight

Next, list ways in which you successfully interact with people. These will be verbs, like the following:

- teach
- produce
- help
- lead
- motivate

- inspire
- manage
- love
- educate
- coach

Finally, visualize what your perfect world would be. What would people do or say? Describe it in writing. Here's an example: "To me, a perfect world is where God's love is the most powerful influence in every life and relationship and Jesus is the role model for all leaders."

Now combine two of your nouns, two of your verbs, and your picture of a perfect world. You'll have a good start on a definition of your life purpose. For example, here's mine: "My life purpose is to use my communication skills and people skills to inspire and help others to make God's love the most powerful influence in their lives and relationships, and to make Jesus their leadership role model."

Pause & Reflect

- As I did, answer the questions in the previous exercise. Pulling them together, what is your personal purpose statement?

SUCCESS AMID SETBACKS

One of the greatest services a family leader can provide is consistency of purpose. When the going gets rough or temptations and distractions come with short-term success or setbacks, family members look to their leaders to see how they'll respond. Will they stay on course and remain true to their purpose, or will they give up or give in to the pressures of the moment?

Think about the intense moments during the evening before Christ's crucifixion. Ponder the depth of character and the love Jesus displayed for His disciples, who within hours would abandon and deny Him. He didn't give in to the temptation to despair over their slowness to grasp the essence of what He'd repeatedly taught them about leading.

As the ultimate servant leader, Jesus demonstrated His willingness to provide what the disciples needed most to grow and develop in their ability to fulfill their purpose. As family leaders, in His strength, we can do the same.

Prayers for Consistency of Purpose

Lord, show me how to prepare for my day in ways that will help me focus on my children's hearts—not just their actions.

Lord, show me what's getting me frustrated and give me Your wisdom on how to deal with every situation—either childish or intentional.

Lord, help me push my ego, pride, and fears aside when my children need discipline and correction. Give me the willingness to teach in that moment, instead of trying to make myself look good.

Lord, as I go through the day taking care of my child's material needs, remind me that it's the heart I must work on.

O Lord, teach me how You want me to parent these girls. Help me through this time of teenhood. Teach me how to lead them to be the women of God You want them to be.

—CAREN, mother of two

Philippians 1:6 says, "He who began a good work in you will complete it." This is a verse that became my prayer during my kids' teen years. I only wish I'd started praying it earlier. It's so encouraging to remember that God started something good in each of my children and that He is working in their lives to complete what He started; it's not just up to me to make them become responsible, mature adults.

—BETH, mother of four

Points to Ponder about the *Head* of Leading Like Jesus as a Parent

- The journey of servant leadership as a parent starts in the heart and must then travel through the head, which is the parent's belief system and perspective on his or her role as a leader.

- A compelling vision tells people who they are, where they are going, and what will guide their journey.

- Once your family's vision is set, you can establish goals to answer the question, "What do you want your family to focus on now?"

- Before trying to influence and engage your family in working with you to create a compelling vision, you need to be clear about your own personal purpose.

- Parental servant leadership starts with a vision and ends with a servant heart that helps family members live according to their values and accomplish agreed-upon goals.

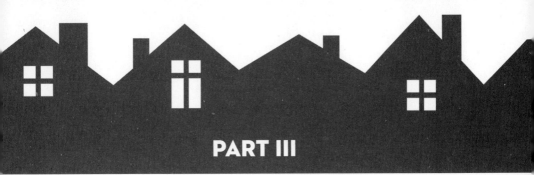

PART III

THE HANDS

Family members will experience what's in your *heart* and *head* when your motivations and beliefs about parenting affect your *hands*—your actions. If as a parent you have a servant heart and a servant-leadership point of view, you'll become a performance coach.

In Chapter Seven, Tricia focuses on making the most of the fleeting parenting years. In Chapter Eight, Ken shows how to be an effective coach. And Phil emphasizes the results of great parenting in Chapter Nine.

SEVEN

For a Limited Time Only

PRINCIPLE 7

To Lead Like Jesus, Make the Most of the Childrearing Years

*Just as Jesus' season of earthly leadership was limited to the span
of a few years, so is our most active season of parenting. In this
chapter Tricia discusses the importance of allowing God to direct
our service to our kids during this brief but intense period.*

It was a typical Thursday—"Library Day" around the Goyer home. I'd rushed
the kids through their chores; it was time to drive them to our local library.

Leslie, age seven, was looking for her shoes. Cory, three years older, was trying to find a book he'd been reading and had set down somewhere. The youngest, Nathan—*where was Nathan?* The quiet one, he often slipped to a side room
with a few toys to sit down and play.

"Kids, we have to get going," I said. "Get your shoes, *now!*" My voice was
anything but kind. "If you don't hurry we won't have time to check out books
before Leslie's piano lessons." I ran to the bathroom to run a brush through my
hair. With that done, I nearly tripped at the top of the stairs on a pile of laundry
I'd been taking down when the phone rang. Leslie ran down the stairs with
shoes in hand and glanced back at me, as if waiting for me to bark more instructions. I grabbed the laundry and under it, found the missing book.

"Cory!" my voice echoed. "Seriously, you guys need to put your things away!
Now hurry, hurry!" I caught an image of myself in a hall mirror as I rushed by—
hair still frazzled, nerves even more so, weighed down with laundry and books.

Tomorrow, I told myself. *I'll get more organized, be more patient tomorrow.* But as soon as that thought filtered through my mind a new one grabbed it by the tail and followed. *This is what they'll remember: today. Do I want all my kids' memories to be like this?*

At that moment I knew I needed to make changes. As a mom with three little kids at home, I would never have my house or schedule or children perfect. Yet I could change my attitude and how I treated the kids. Ten years from now they wouldn't remember the trips to the library or piano lessons, but they'd remember how they were treated. I didn't want most of their childhood memories to feature a frantic, cranky mom. Did I want my home to be a place of joy or one of conflict? I had a choice.

If my child's most vivid memory was of the day she just lived, she would remember me as a serving parent. Last night my family delivered a hot meal plus a toiletry bag to four families in our community who are in need. It's our Tuesday night tradition. She would remember that we loved on families who don't always feel loved.

—JENNIFER, mother of two

Pause & Reflect

- If your child's most vivid childhood memory was of today, what would he or she remember?
- Would your child remember you more as a self-serving parent or a serving parent? Why?

The more I thought about my own growing-up years, I realized it wasn't the unusual events that stood out, but the usual ones. They included sitting around the television watching sports or the news as we ate. They involved slipping off to my room to read a book or do homework alone, because time spent playing board games or even talking as a family was unheard of. A parent's attitude, I realized, is the foundation for how every day is lived out. And those days are the building blocks of childhood memories.

THE URGENCY OF JESUS

The Bible tells us that Jesus' season of earthly leadership was limited to a period of roughly three years. It began when He came to be baptized by John the Baptist and ended with His death, resurrection, and ascension into heaven. This followed a period of eighteen years during which Jesus lived and worked in relative obscurity.

How much can one accomplish in three years? A lot, if you make the most of them—and Jesus did. The urgency of His mission didn't cause Him to panic, but it did keep Him from wasting time on nonessentials. Consider these examples:

> Another follower said, "Master, excuse me for a couple of days, please. I have my father's funeral to take care of."
>
> Jesus refused. "First things first. Your business is life, not death. Follow me. Pursue life." (Matthew 8:21-22, MSG)

> Then Jesus made a circuit of all the towns and villages. He taught in their meeting places, reported kingdom news, and healed their diseased bodies, healed their bruised and hurt lives. When he looked out over the crowds, his heart broke. So confused and aimless they were, like sheep with no shepherd. "What a huge harvest!" he said to his disciples. "How few workers! On your knees and pray for harvest hands!"
>
> The prayer was no sooner prayed than it was answered. Jesus called twelve of his followers and sent them into the ripe fields. He gave them

power to kick out the evil spirits and to tenderly care for the bruised and hurt lives. . . .

Jesus sent his twelve harvest hands out with this charge:

"Don't begin by traveling to some far-off place to convert unbelievers. And don't try to be dramatic by tackling some public enemy. Go to the lost, confused people right here in the neighborhood. Tell them that the kingdom is here. Bring health to the sick. Raise the dead. Touch the untouchables. Kick out the demons. You have been treated generously, so live generously.

"Don't think you have to put on a fund-raising campaign before you start. You don't need a lot of equipment. *You* are the equipment, and all you need to keep that going is three meals a day. Travel light. . . .

"Stay alert. This is hazardous work I'm assigning you. You're going to be like sheep running through a wolf pack, so don't call attention to yourselves. Be as cunning as a snake, inoffensive as a dove." (Matthew 9:35–10:1, 5-16, MSG)

Jesus knew how brief His "window" of earthly ministry would be, and led His followers accordingly. We don't know that much about our own futures, but a little math makes it clear that our most active parenting years are few.

How can we make the most of that season?

The following are four ways to avoid wasting those precious parenting moments.

WAY #1: VALUE EVERY DAY

No one wants to go through a near-death experience, but that's what happened to my friend Ocieanna. This young mom of four was having an ordinary Saturday night when her heart stopped. One minute she was watching television with her husband; the next she gasped, gagged, and slumped over with no pulse.

I heard about it the next day when another friend contacted me. When I got the news, Ocieanna had been put into an induced coma and her body was being chilled to try to minimize the damage. The doctors weren't sure she was going to make it, and my heart went out to her husband and four young kids.

Prayers went out all over the world. Despite the fact that her heart stopped a second time, less than a week later she came to. Ocieanna was confused, but everyone knew she was going to be all right when her friends and family were gathered in her hospital room and she started introducing those who hadn't met each other.

I never would have called Ocieanna a self-serving parent. Yet I can say that her near-death experience brought change. She cut out activities and has more down time with her kids. She's less stressed about her housework and more focused on her family.

Recently Ocieanna and I were writing a novel together. When I mentioned one day that we had a lot to do and not nearly enough time, she sent me a quick note: "I'm not worried about it. I almost died, and I make a point of not worrying about these things."

Her words calmed my heart. Each day—even busy, tiring, emotional days with our kids—is a day we need to be thankful for.

Pause & Reflect

- Has there been a time in your life when you "saw the light" and realized how short the active parenting years are? What brought about that revelation?
- What changes took place in your heart? Your head? Your hands?

WAY #2: PAY ATTENTION TO GOD'S NUDGES

I'll be the first to admit that for many years I was more of a self-serving leader than a servant leader. We're all self-serving to some extent in certain situations and relationships, of course; even a person everyone applauds as a servant leader will have moments when his or her ego gets in the way.

But when the season of parenting slips by so quickly, we can't afford to waste it on self-centeredness. Fortunately, no case is hopeless. God can get our attention in at least two ways, helping self-serving family leaders begin to make efforts to serve rather than be served.

The first way is by having a near-death experience—as my aforementioned friend Ocieanna did. Interestingly, when people know they've been given a second chance and are on borrowed time, they seem to mellow. It's the "Scrooge" phenomenon. When people get in touch with their own mortality, they often see things differently and start to realize that life is more about what you give than what you get—more about serving than being served.

A second way people begin to see their lives and parenting differently is through a spiritual awakening. That's why the authors of this book are so committed to inspiring and equipping people to lead like Jesus in their homes. That transformation can't take place without developing a relationship with Jesus. When people start walking with Him, He calls them to shed their self-serving habits and do as He would do.

The story at the beginning of this chapter was a spiritual awakening of sorts for me. I can't tell you how many hundreds of days I'd acted that way as a mom—stressed, impatient, overwhelmed. The thought that popped into my mind—*Is this really how you want your kids to remember their home life?*—wasn't something I came up with. I'm certain it was a prodding of the Holy Spirit. I can't say everything changed after that day, but I did begin to look at things differently. I realized I wanted to create a home life that my kids could look back on with joy.

After that day I started praying about my attitude. I prayed I would have the heart of a joyful servant. I prayed I would worry less about the mess and hurry, and smile and treat my kids with love and respect.

That day was an *aha* moment. I believe God saw something that needed to change and He chose that moment to reach down and tap me on the shoulder. I could have pushed that thought from my mind, but deep down I had a feeling He was the One speaking. The more I've learned to heed that voice that comes up with wisdom beyond myself, the more joy and peace I've found in my home.

Now my older kids are ages twenty-three, twenty, and eighteen. When they talk about their younger years, they focus more on the fun times than the stress—glory be to God. We also have jumped into the parenting years the second time around by adopting a baby girl who's two years old at this writing. By heeding God's still, small voice through the years, I've become far more of a servant-parent this time around—better equipped to make the most of this second-chance opportunity.

Pause & Reflect

- **When was the last time God reached down and tapped you on the shoulder as a parent? What did He seem to say to your heart?**
- **Did you heed His still, small voice? What was the result?**

I became a believer in Christ as an adult. One Sunday at church there was a presentation on mission trips. I felt called to serve. Since that Sunday, each summer I have been on a mission trip. And now I am involved in a local mission ministry to serve the folks living in our community. I have changed from a person who didn't like people to be in my personal space to a woman who loves to love on people! And it's all because Christ changed my heart.

—Jennifer, mother of two

After going toe-to-toe with my youngest daughter, I was frustrated. The only thing I seemed to be able to change was her behavior—and not her heart—towards her disobedience. God tapped me on the shoulder during church and changed how I saw mothering. Instead of assuming and demanding obedience because I was her mom, God whispered to my heart how to capture my child's heart and empower her to make better choices. It's not the behavior I want to change, it's her heart.

—HEATHER, mother of three

WAY #3: GET A MENTOR TO HELP

Here's a third factor that can help you make the most of your parenting years: having a significant role model. When you're around a servant-leadership role model often enough, his or her behavior begins to rub off. Mentoring is something many overlook during the parenting years. But everyone needs it, especially when it accelerates your progress in dealing with the challenges of parenting.

When my son was born, I had so many questions and concerns. I was only seventeen when I gave birth to Cory, but I wanted to be the best mom possible. Starting to attend church, I met a lady named Cheryl. I never asked her to be my mentor; I watched her. I studied the way she lovingly interacted with her kids. I noticed that they knew Bible stories better than I did. I took mental notes on how I could parent better.

As the years passed, Cheryl was only one of many women I looked up to. I got close to some older moms and asked their advice, but most of the time I just watched and applied what I thought would work with my kids. It saved time and tears when I didn't have to reinvent the parenting wheel.

I also discovered that I didn't have to be perfect to *be* a mentor. A wise woman once told me, "Every mother should have those you look ahead to, those you walk beside, and those who you offer your wisdom to." For years I didn't think I had enough wisdom to offer, but then I started serving teenage mothers. Any help I could give was help they didn't have. It made me strive to be a better role model as I parented my own kids. After all, I now had people watching me, following me.

Pause & Reflect

> • Who is someone you can look up to as a parent? How could that make it easier to deal with the brevity of the parenting years?
> • Who is someone you can help as he or she struggles in the parenting journey? What's one bit of time-saving wisdom you could share?

We are blessed to have a couple we look up to as parents—in faith, education methods, and in family decisions. As relatively new parents ourselves, we can reach out in love to other new parents, special needs parents, and couples or singles who are not yet parents. We can offer good examples, support through mistakes (our own included), and encouragement.

—Caroline and Joey, parents of two

I look up to Marcy, the mom of a childhood friend of mine from elementary school. She was always a passionate mom who loved God and had fun with life. God came easily into conversation, praise songs were common, and all heavy matters were immediately turned over to a "Dad who loves us more than we can imagine." Her unconventional approaches to relationship with God and others inspire me and make my marriage and my parenting better.

—Wendy, mother of four

I have a friend that I meet with every Friday to pray with as my prayer partner. . . .

[My husband and I are] struggling with our oldest son, who has left home and is making poor decisions, but those decisions are his own and are not a reflection of who we are. I'm sure there are those in our community who might be tempted to say, "Oh, those people need help. What is that kid

up to?" But there are many more in the community who know us and
recognize that we do know what we're doing. (Our other kids love God
and are on the right track. . . .)

My point is that you have something to teach to anyone and everyone
has something you can learn from. The family that needs extra care and
help right now doesn't want my condescension, but rather my acceptance.

—AMY, mother of four

WAY #4: PINPOINT YOUR CHILD'S
DEVELOPMENT LEVEL

In *The Servant Leader*, Ken and Phil discuss Situational Leadership® II, a way to diagnose people's development levels. By using this system to measure a child's development level regarding a particular goal or task, parents can be far more effective—a great head start when the active parenting years are so short.

Here's how that works.

As you probably know, you can't treat all your kids the same way. It's also true that each child needs to be treated differently depending on the task or goal at hand. To know how to treat each child, we need to consider two components: competence and commitment. For this discussion, let's call them *ability* and *willingness*.

Ability is a child's capacity to do something. Children who are able in a particular area have the knowledge, skill, and experience to do tasks in that area without direction from others. For example, they might say, "Opening the door and handing out bulletins is something I can do at church without help from my mom or dad."

Willingness is a child's motivation and confidence to do something. Children who are willing to do something in a particular area think that area is important; they display confidence and good feelings about themselves. They don't need a pat on the back to get things done. They could say something like,

"It makes me feel good to help with the songs in vacation Bible school. I love the music and the hand motions, and I can tell the younger kids really enjoy it, too."

There are four ways to combine these two factors of ability and willingness:

1. Children who have *low ability but high willingness* to take responsibility for their own behavior in a particular area are Enthusiastic Beginners because they have never done this task before. For example: A fifteen-year-old teenager, the day she gets her learner's permit to drive. She is filled with excitement and confidence, but knows little about driving.

2. Children with *low to some ability but low willingness* are Disillusioned Learners because they either had some failure during the learning process or realized that the task was harder than they thought. For example: A teenager becoming nervous as cars honk their horns and try to pass her during her first drive on the highway.

3. Children who have *moderate to high ability but variable willingness* are Capable but Cautious Performers because they may have lost some of their enthusiasm or confidence or are cautious in performing the task on their own. For example: A teenager getting nervous and failing her driving test, even though she got an A in driver's education.

4. Children with both *high ability and high willingness* are Self-Reliant Achievers because they are experienced and highly motivated to perform a particular task. For example: A teenager passing her driver's test with flying colors and being permitted to drive herself to school every day.

Even though your kids might not be teenagers, hopefully these descriptions will help you recognize your children's development level. Pinpointing your child's development level can put you on a fast track to helping your children become Self-Reliant Achievers in various parts of their lives—and to be more patient with them when they aren't.

It also saves you trial-and-error time when you as a parent understand your own development level.

For instance, there are times when I'm willing but not able: "I would love to lead family devotions, but I wish someone would help me find the time in my schedule. And even when I do sit down with everything, the baby usually makes it impossible for us to get anything accomplished."

There are times when I have some ability but lack the motivation: "When I started doing family devotions with our kids, I found it was easier said than done. I became a little discouraged."

There are times when I'm able but my willingness wavers: "I have a great devotional book, and my kids love it, but if I don't get on my exercise bike first thing in the morning my exercise just doesn't get done."

And thank goodness there are times when I'm both able and willing: "I hear You speaking to my heart, God, and I have the perfect devotional book. I'm going to start today by reading a family devotion during our dinnertime."

The best part is that no matter what development level we or our children have attained, God is there to help us. If we hear His still, small voice urging us to change, that doesn't mean He expects us to do it all on our own. It's not like He's sitting up in heaven with His arms crossed over His chest, saying, "You sure do have a big problem there. Let's see how you're going to fix it."

Despite the brevity of the parenting season, we don't need to strive or worry or fear. Instead, we need to turn to God for help. This isn't the first time we've quoted the following passage in this book, and it won't be the last:

> *Do not be anxious about anything, but in everything,*
> *by prayer and petition, with thanksgiving, present your*
> *requests to God. And the peace of God, which transcends*
> *all understanding, will guard your hearts and your*
> *minds in Christ Jesus. (Philippians 4:6-7)*

God not only wants to direct our transformation, He wants to achieve it through His wisdom and power. "Lord, show me how I need to change, and then work to change me," is a prayer He always answers with a *yes*.

THAT CHAMPIONSHIP SEASON

Through God's transformation in my heart, mentoring, and learning from people like my friend Ocieanna, my self-serving attitude has undergone many changes over the years. Additional attitude adjustments have come as I've understood what hands-on parenting is all about. It's a season in life. It's a tough season at times, but kids grow into adults. I've witnessed that myself. What I'm dealing with today with my kids won't be what I'm dealing with next year or even next week.

As with any home improvement project, small steps in parenting can lead to big changes. Marriage is for life, and hands-on parenting is for a season. But the influence of parenting endures even after the hands-on work is done.

With three children on the autism spectrum, I have definite parenting challenges. I have been struggling with trying to be gentler with them but at the same time hold them accountable for their actions. The more I try to be gentle in my own strength, the harsher I become. I really need to lean on God more, not only during the challenging situations, but before they even start. I need to spend more time in the Word and praying for my children and myself as their caregiver.

—MICHELLE, mother of five

I am a learned worrier, and I ache to trust God instead of worry. My worry only stresses and harms my family. Much of this worry results from trying to do things in my own strength rather than remembering He is over all. I can and should turn my parenting to Him in prayer—prayer for my children, for our futures, for forgiveness of and redeeming my mistakes. Memorizing Scripture has helped me to renew my heart to Him when I find myself in the middle of worry.

—CAROLINE, mother of two

Pause & Reflect

- In what area of your life are you most trying to develop as a parent? What's your development level in that area?
- Are you trying to be a Self-Reliant Achiever, or are you turning it over to God? How would the latter look?
- When people say that the hands-on parenting season is over "before you know it," do you feel skeptical, sad, hopeful, worried, or glad? How could Philippians 4:6-7 help?

EIGHT

Teaching to the Test

PRINCIPLE 8
To Lead Like Jesus, Help Kids Succeed

Once you, as a family leader, have an inspiring vision for your family, how can you help your kids live accordingly? As Ken shows in this chapter, hands-on coaching—with a servant's heart—is the most effective way to help them be all you want them to be.

When I was a college professor, I was periodically in trouble with the faculty. That's because at the beginning of the class, I often handed my students the final exam. When the other teachers found out about that, they asked, "What are you *doing?*"

"I'm confused," I'd tell them. "I thought we were supposed to teach our students."

"We are. But don't give them the final exam ahead of time!"

I'd smile. "Not only will I give them the final exam on the first day of class, but what do you think I'm going to do all semester? I'm going to teach them the answers, so when they get to the final exam, they'll get As."

Life is all about getting As—not maintaining a normal distribution curve. I wanted all my students to win. That's exactly what Jesus wants—all of us to win. He never believed in a normal distribution curve. He wanted everyone to win and become His disciples.

HOW JESUS COACHED

Leading your family like Jesus means changing your parenting behavior to be more like that of Jesus. It means asking yourself, "What would Jesus do?" before you act as the family's leader. This is particularly true when it comes to your parental role as a hands-on performance coach.

When Jesus called His disciples to follow Him, He pledged them His full support and guidance as they developed into "fishers of men." This is the duty of family servant leaders—the ongoing investment of their time and energy in the lives of those who follow, especially their children.

Parents wanting to become effective family coaches must understand that there are three parts to performance coaching: performance planning, day-to-day coaching, and performance evaluation.

Performance planning is all about providing direction and setting goals. In many ways it's the visionary or leadership aspect of servant leadership.

Once you, as a parent, establish clear goals for your children, your role switches from performance planning to *day-to-day coaching*. This is the implementation or servant aspect of servant leadership—helping your children accomplish their goals.

As the diagram on the next page depicts, when you move into servant mode the traditional pyramid hierarchy must be turned upside-down. Now the children you are attempting to coach are at the top, where they can be *responsible*— able to respond—and perform. In this scenario, you as a parent move to the bottom of the pyramid, where you serve and are *responsive* to the needs of your children—training and developing them so they can accomplish established goals and live according to your family vision.

When Jesus washed the feet of His disciples, He was switching His focus from the visionary/direction role of servant leadership (the leadership aspect) to the implementation role (the servant aspect). As He did that, He turned the pyramid upside-down. In the process, He demonstrated the true essence of servant leadership and challenged His disciples to do the same.

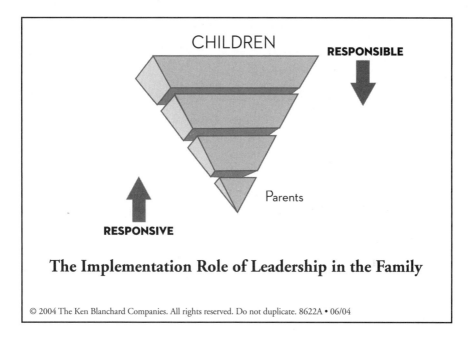

The Implementation Role of Leadership in the Family

Remember what Jesus said after He washed the disciples' feet?

After he had finished washing their feet, he took his robe, put it back on, and went back to his place at the table.

Then he said, "Do you understand what I have done to you? You address me as 'Teacher' and 'Master,' and rightly so. That is what I am. So if I, the Master and Teacher, washed your feet, you must now wash each other's feet. I've laid down a pattern for you. What I've done, you do. I'm only pointing out the obvious. A servant is not ranked above his master; an employee doesn't give orders to the employer. If you understand what I'm telling you, act like it—and live a blessed life." (John 13:12-17, MSG)

Jesus didn't send His disciples out to serve without clear direction. He didn't imply that they should go out and help people do whatever they wanted. The vision was clear. He got it from the top of the hierarchy—His Father.

As "fishers of men," His followers were to "go and make disciples of all nations," focusing first on loving God and then on loving their neighbors

(Matthew 4:19; 28:19; 22:37-40). To carry out this vision, Jesus empowered His disciples to be servant leaders who helped others understand and believe the good news. He was a great day-to-day coach.

That leads to the third part of performance coaching, *performance evaluation*. This requires sitting down with people and examining their behavior over time.

Though Jesus was no longer with His disciples in body, He was still present in spirit and in His teachings. By becoming "fishers of men" in the years after Jesus' return to heaven, His disciples proved that when it comes to effective performance coaching, *the most important thing is not what happens when you're there, but what happens when you're not.*

I think the same goes for our kids. We won't always be around. Hopefully, however, we'll instill in our children the ability and willingness to follow God's Word and depend on His guidance in their everyday lives.

We create small jobs for the little ones that they are capable of doing well. These are given first, with a slightly harder job to push them a bit. When the inevitable "I can't do it" comes out, we remind them of the times they persevered and did get something done they didn't believe they could do before. That usually lights the fire under them to keep trying. We follow through on what we say we are going to do, too.

—ALLISON, mother of three

I can create an atmosphere of mutual service and trust in my home when I remember that I am here to protect, guide, and show my kids the reality of Christ, not just control them or the environment around them. I also create trust when I see my kids' thoughts as worthwhile and each moment with them as a gift. Gratitude helps me hold on to a positive attitude full of love and respect!

—CAROLINE, mother of two

Having a very independent, strong-willed daughter, I learned early on that the sooner I could remove myself from the equation, the more smoothly things will go. So if I want her to cook dinner, I don't stand over her and give her directions. Instead, I let her pick the menu and the recipe and give her control of the kitchen. When she has a question or needs my help, she'll come ask.

—DIANE, mother of two

HOW PERFORMANCE COACHING WORKS IN THE FAMILY

As I've mentioned, there are three parts to performance coaching:

1. Performance planning
2. Day-to-day coaching
3. Performance evaluation

Performance coaching starts with performance planning, where clear goals are set up front. In fact, the first secret of *The One Minute Manager* is *goal setting.* All good performance starts from clear goals.

The second secret of *The One Minute Manager* is *praising progress.* To set children up for praise, it's vitally important that parents be clear up front with their kids about what good behavior looks like in various aspects of their lives. If good behavior is well defined, parents can move to day-to-day coaching and praise any progress.

If progress isn't being made, parents can reprimand or redirect their kids' energy to keep them on track. That's essentially what the third secret of *The One Minute Manager* is all about: *redirection.*

Performance planning and day-to-day coaching go together; both are keys to goal accomplishment. Day-to-day coaching keeps performance on track. But without clear goals, you have nothing to "coach about." Margie and I realized this when we helped our kids Scott and Debbie with their schoolwork. When it came to academic performance goals, we wanted them to achieve at least a 3.0 or B average. We felt that those grades, combined with participating in school activities and student leadership positions, could get them into good colleges.

You might wonder why we didn't insist that they be straight-A students. We believed "all work and no play make Johnny a dull boy." We wanted them to gain some social skills as well as academic ones.

Once we'd established goals in these areas, we set up day-to-day coaching by doing everything we could to monitor our kids' progress and guide them toward success. For instance, we found out that teachers had to fill out a progress report every Friday for students who were having academic problems. Even if your child wasn't having trouble, as a parent you could ask that the weekly report be done for your child. So Margie and I asked for those reports. Scott and Debbie didn't like that very much, but it gave us a real way to monitor their progress.

By learning how our kids were doing in school, Margie and I were able to help them succeed and participate in their success. It also provided the information we needed to praise progress and/or redirect their efforts. While the kids weren't great students—just as Margie and I weren't—they did well enough to get into good colleges.

Debbie graduated from the University of Colorado. Scott got interested in hotel administration and hospitality. Although Cornell had the best school for that, he couldn't get in there directly. The people in the Cornell admissions department said that if he went somewhere else and did well, he could be admitted. So Scott went to the University of Las Vegas for a year and transferred to Cornell in his sophomore year.

I'll never forget the conversation we had when he was driving to Cornell in his big truck with his dog, Nero. He called me on the phone and asked, "Dad, why am I doing this? I like UNLV."

"Scott, you could have gotten just as good a classroom education at UNLV, if not better," I told him. "The difference in going to Cornell is that the kids dream bigger dreams. That's the value of going to a school that's hard to get into. People have good self-images."

He called me again about a month and a half later. "Dad, I get what you were saying about big dreams. What I've discovered here is that at UNLV the students used to dream about running a Sheraton. At Cornell they talk about having their own hotel chain."

Soon, though, Scott got into a fraternity—and the partying. He wasn't doing as well academically as he should have been, so they asked him to take a semester off. When he came home at the end of the fall semester, Margie and I were waiting for him at the door.

"Scott," we said, "come on into the bedroom. We want to talk to you."

Rather than just redirecting his efforts—which is appropriate when someone is still learning how to do something—we gave him the following one-minute reprimand: "We just want to tell you that we're really disappointed in your academic performance. Essentially, you 'busted out' of school. The reason we're disappointed is that you're a better student than that. We know you can do better. That's all we wanted to say. We won't discuss this anymore on your vacation. You know where we stand."

We gave him a hug, and that was it for the vacation. With a reprimand, you don't keep bringing it up. You say it once and find ways to observe behavior and praise progress again.

I did take one action, though. A friend, Bob Small, was one of the great hoteliers in America. He'd built five-star hotels for Marriott and the Bass Brothers in Texas, as well as the new hotels at Disney. He later became president of the Fairmont Hotels, with their crown jewel in San Francisco. During the semester break I called Bob.

"I've got an intern for you," I said, and told him about Scott.

"Send him down—we'll shape him up," Bob said.

The time Scott spent with Bob at the Worthington Hotel in Fort Worth, Texas, was a marvelous experience. To this day Scott calls Bob "Mr. Small" because he learned so much from him. Scott returned to Cornell the next fall, ready to work hard and graduate—which he did. Scott loves to point to his framed diploma because it says, "Be it known . . . that Kenneth Scott Blanchard graduated from Cornell University."

Not only did Scott and Debbie graduate from college, but when they decided they wanted to work in our company, they also got their master's degrees in organizational development and change at American University in Washington, D.C. These successes were all possible because we set clear academic goals and followed up those goals with day-to-day coaching, praising progress, and redirecting or reprimanding performance that was off course. That's what being a hands-on coach is all about.

Coaching is the most important servant-leadership element of parenting. Once goals are clear, servant-hearted parents are available on a day-to-day basis to help their children win—by accomplishing stated goals. I can't emphasize enough that day-to-day coaching, or the servant aspect of servant leadership, can be effective only if the visionary work and clear goal setting are done first.

Pause & Reflect

- Do you initiate coaching? If so, how? If not, what are you waiting for?
- When was the last time you coached your kids? How did you do it?
- Would you call your coaching "hands-on"? Why or why not?
- What are the lessons you're currently trying to teach your children? How could you help them "pass the final exam"?
- Family leadership is not about power or control; it's about helping your children win. What's the next thing you'll do to help them accomplish established goals and become independent, responsible family members?

It's always a struggle between "It's just easier to do it myself" and knowing that I need to be teaching and equipping my children to be responsible adults. The more responsibility I give them, the more I see them stretching out of their comfort zones and overcoming obstacles.

—DIANE, mother of two

As a mother of a toddler and a newborn, day-to-day coaching literally is a part of our daily lives. I instruct, guide, redirect, and praise throughout the day with my toddler son. I praise my son for his efforts or explain why he should or shouldn't take a certain action, like using bad words or not hitting when he's frustrated.

—CAROLINE, mother of two

My job as a mom has been to cultivate character and build interest, much like wrapping up a beautiful package with shimmering ribbon that holds the perfect gift for God—my child's heart.

I want my kids to know that God is eager for them to have a relationship with Him and He has been invested in their lives from day one. Each of my children has their individual name on their bedroom wall, followed by, "Before you were born I knew you. Jeremiah 1:5." This saying was the first thing my youngest daughter looked at as she lay on her changing table getting her diaper changed. Now she looks at this saying above her desk as she colors in her coloring books or practices writing her name. To help her, I point to her name on the wall, "Alexa, A-L-E-X-A, before you were born God knew you." She smiles and writes, not realizing that the most important truth I want her to know is pressed into her heart as tangibly as she touches her crayon to the paper.

—WENDY, mother of four

SOME PITFALLS WITH PARENTAL COACHING

Of the three parts to performance coaching—performance planning, day-to-day coaching, and performance evaluation—which one do you think gets the most attention from managers in organizations? Most people guess performance evaluation. Unfortunately, they're right. It's true of parents as well.

Why? Because most parents don't set clear goals with their kids, even though they usually have in mind a sense of what they want them to focus on. For example, in guiding the academic achievements of their children, a lot of parents don't set goals and objectives until after the kids bring home what they don't want. They'll see their kids' report cards and move straight to performance evaluation, exploding, "I can't believe these Cs and Ds! You've got to be kidding me!" Now all of a sudden they're setting goals after the fact.

This leads to what we call the "bring me a rock" syndrome. It occurs when a parent issues a nonspecific instruction like "Bring me a rock," but fails to test for understanding and becomes annoyed with results that don't meet his or her expectations. What kind of rock did the parent want? When was the child to bring it?

Another way would-be parental coaches get into trouble occurs when their kids become teenagers and should begin making responsible decisions on their own. The trouble comes when parents, still wanting to be in charge, take control of every aspect of their teen's life.

For example, suppose a teenager is upset with the parent's over-supervision of his friendships. The teenager storms out of the house saying, "I'm sick and tired of everything having to be your way. I'm out of here! I wish I didn't have to come back!"

Parents who don't get the servant aspect of servant leadership might run to the door and yell, "Who do you think you're talking to, young man? Get back here this minute!" That approach would result in a lose-lose power struggle. As *The Living Bible* paraphrases Ephesians 6:4:

> *And now a word to you parents. Don't keep on scolding*
> *and nagging your children, making them angry and resentful.*
> *Rather, bring them up with loving discipline the Lord himself*
> *approves, with suggestions and godly advice.*

A parent who understands servant leadership and loving discipline might go to the door and call after the teenager, "I see that you're angry and resentful, and it looks like I might be one of the reasons. Could we talk tonight?" The body language of the teenager will completely change, because his parent has reached out to serve rather than condemn.

If you're seeking to lead your family like Jesus, your vision always should be *committed service to the best interests of the other person*. That means responding to and encouraging the best in others without exploiting knowledge of their weaknesses and shortcomings for your own purposes—or catering to whims and individual preferences.

The topic of drinking alcohol came up recently with my preteens. We discussed when drinking is allowed and what responsibility looks like. We also watched an episode of Intervention *to see what the consequences of drinking can lead to. We then talked about other things in our lives that can control us if not kept in check.*

—CAREN, mother of two

For hands-on coaching we praise the little things our kids do as well as the big things. We tell our children, often, how proud we are. When they make good choices, we praise. When they make poor decisions, we talk about them without tearing down the child. We help them see how those choices didn't line up with God's Word, or how Jesus lived.

—ALLISON, mother of three

Confidence and trust in the Lord are things that we teach our children and that we live by. It doesn't mean that they are confident before they start anything—I'm not either, sometimes. It means that we can have the tools to move forward. It makes me so happy to see their smiles when they do their part and they trust in God for help with little things and big things. I feel like my mission is being accomplished.

—FERNANDA, mother of two

I try to model good behavior, but of course I'm imperfect at doing so!
Even imperfect modeling can turn into good modeling when I claim
my mistakes and demonstrate turning to God for both forgiveness and
guidance.

—Caroline, mother of two

HOW JESUS WAS COACHED

There was nothing random in the life of Jesus. This includes learning the carpenter craft from His earthly father in preparation for His season of earthly leadership.

It's interesting to note that when Jesus returned to His hometown of Nazareth, people quickly identified him as "the carpenter" and "the son of the carpenter." The unremarkable nature of His local reputation would indicate that the way He learned and went about His craft wasn't out of the ordinary.

Joseph would have coached Jesus through the stages of learning. Under the instruction of His father, Jesus would have progressed from novice to apprentice to journeyman, and finally to master teacher. Through the day-to-day coaching, the transfer of knowledge and wisdom flowed from one generation to the next.

When Jesus was a novice, Joseph would have given Him basic orientation to being a carpenter—including how, where, when, and why He was to do certain things. As Jesus worked with Joseph as an apprentice, Joseph would have acted as a performance coach, showing Him the right way to do things to produce the right results. Joseph would have given Jesus instruction, observed His behavior, provided support and encouragement, and redirected Him as necessary in the tasks assigned.

When Jesus was a journeyman, able to work on His own, Joseph would have assigned Him tasks and then would have become His head cheerleader and supporter. When Jesus became a master teacher, demonstrating His competence in all the key aspects of His craft, Joseph would have changed his leadership to empower Him and send Him out to work on His own.

It's reasonable to assume that Jesus mastered the craft of carpentry. Had it been God's will for Him to teach it to others, He would have done so in obedience and excellence.

What we do know is that Jesus applied His knowledge of obedience to the way He guided His disciples from call to commission. From novices to master teachers, Jesus coached them and sent them out to teach others in His name. It's an example we parents would do well to follow.

Want to help your child learn a skill? Look at the following chart to understand the best kind of leadership to apply in coaching him or her. Select a task or skill you're trying to teach your child. Identify his or her stage of development and what leadership style would be most effective.

LEARNING STAGES

Novice	Apprentice	Journeyman	Master
(someone just starting out)	(someone in training)	(someone able to work on his or her own)	(someone able to teach others)
⬆	⬆	⬆	⬆

LEADER PROVIDES

Instructing	Coaching	Mentoring	Commissioning
Basic information: What, How, Where, When, Why	Instruction, Practice, and Evaluation	Assignment and Encouragement	Affirmation and Autonomy

Pause & Reflect

- Think of a time when you were an untrained novice, just starting to learn a new task or role. What did you need most from someone else to help you get started? Did you get it? If not, what was the result?
- Think of a time when you needed someone to push you beyond a failure or an easy early success to get to a higher level of understanding and performance. What did you learn?
- Think of a time when you quit because nobody was there to take you to the next level. What do you wish had happened?

EVERYBODY WINS

When it comes to coaching, it's important to follow Jesus' model. He was clear about the leadership aspect of servant leadership—why He came, what the good news was, and what He wanted people to do. He modeled the servant aspect of servant leadership with everyone He met. He told His followers, "Go and make disciples of all nations."

Why? Because He wanted everybody to win.

I never really had anyone encouraging me or pushing me to go to college after high school, and subsequently I didn't go. On the other hand, when I joined the Air Force, I had plenty of drill sergeants and supervisors who pushed me! I was surprised to find out that I liked being pushed and I liked the feeling of accomplishment that came with success. I believe God used that time to prepare me. I was not used to boundaries and yet I came to discover that I craved the safety and security they offered. That time prepared me for the day when I would come to embrace His boundaries and His will for my life.

—Diane, mother of two

Steps to Hands-On Coaching

1. Setting the purpose or vision
2. Communicating a compelling picture of the future
3. Defining and modeling the values, structure, and behavior you want from people
4. Creating an environment of empowerment
5. Moving to the bottom of the pyramid
6. Showing respect for everyone
    - Which of these steps are your strengths?
    - Which ones could you learn more about and improve?

NINE

Follow Me

PRINCIPLE 9

To Lead Like Jesus, Inspire Obedience—Not Rebellion

Obedience—an integral part of parenting—means more than just getting your kids to conform to your wishes. In its highest form, it's modeled after the loving obedience Jesus maintained toward His Father. Phil discusses how to parent in a way that will inspire obedience rather than provoke rebellion.

My friend Ed, a wise man and fellow grandpa, recounted a memorable conversation with his teenage son. The son asked his father for permission to drive to another city with friends to attend a concert. Ed said he wasn't convinced it was a good idea, and wouldn't grant his permission.

The son responded with a familiar teenage question: "Why won't you let me go? Is it because you don't trust me?"

Instead of rising to the bait, Ed asked his son a question of his own. "Son, can you ever remember a time when I haven't had your best interest at heart?"

After thinking for a moment, his son lowered his head. "I can't think of a time."

Ed then posed a second question. "So, Son, the question that needs to be answered is not whether I trust you—but rather, when did you stop trusting me?"

Ed stayed firm on his decision. His son left unhappy, but had learned a lesson about trust and obedience.

NOTE FROM A NEWBORN

If cuddling with kids and watching Disney movies while eating popcorn is one of the easiest parts of being a parent, teaching kids obedience is one of the hardest. Not only is it hard; we also feel unappreciated in the process. No, more than that, we feel like the bad guy. Maybe things would be easier if we received a letter like this before the hard years of parenting started:

Dear Mom and Dad,

Thank you for the gift of life. I am grateful that you believed in my potential to be a blessing to you and to the people I will meet during my lifetime. I thank God for placing you in my life.

Whatever happens from this moment forward, one thing will never change. I am your child and you are my parents, forever. You will always be the living images of the words "Father" and "Mother" that I carry with me all the days of my life. Whatever you teach me about love and what is important in life will mold my view of who I am and my view of the world.

Before things get too hectic, I want to thank you in advance for the sacrifices you will make on my behalf so that I may grow into the person God intends me to be. Thank you for all the busy days and sleepless nights that you will invest in caring for my needs. Thank you for praying for wisdom in how to guide me through all the pain and mistakes I will experience as I grow. Thank you for standing firm when I test your patience so that I may learn obedience.

Thank you for your encouragement and discipline. Thank you for listening to me even when my arguments don't make sense and my frustrations spill over. Thank you for letting me fail, when failure is the best teacher and humility is the lesson. Thank you for picking me up and dusting me off when I fall, so I will not be discouraged as I learn.

Thank you for all the times you will comfort me with the hugs and kisses that always make things better. Thank you for cleaning up the messes I make, and then teaching me how to clean them up myself. Thank you for teaching me to value what is important to God. Thank you for teaching me that love includes forgiveness, compassion, apologies, accountability, as well as patience, kindness, generosity, humility, courtesy, good temper, unselfishness, grace, and sincerity. Thank you for saying no when what I ask is not in my best interest. Thank you for enduring my seasons of rebellion that will come with the growing pains of becoming an adult.

Thank you for making it easier to obey you by keeping the rules simple, the consequences consistent, the standards for success attainable, praising my progress, explaining why, and most of all, modeling the behaviors and attitudes you want me to develop.

My prayer is that God will bless you with the wisdom and the courage to raise me in such a way that I will grow to understand what it means to have faith in the love of God, to believe in His Word, and to obey His commandments.

Love,

Your Precious Child

"I CAN'T WANNA DO IT!"

We'll never get a letter like that. But it helps to know that our efforts will pay off. If we strive to bring our children to obedience they'll learn not only to obey us—and be a beneficial part of our family—but also learn to obey God and be a beneficial part of *His* family.

Obedience is first and foremost a matter of the heart. It can be described as an internal desire to willingly respond in trust and respect when called to action. It involves wanting to do what's required. Obedience is not a natural response of our hearts or the hearts of our children. It cannot be forced or coerced; it must be nurtured as a choice.

Obedience goes beyond compliance and conformity. There's a strong temptation to measure the success of our parenting by the external behavior of our children: If they do what they're told, say their prayers, stop rolling their eyes every time we ask them to do something, exhibit good manners outside the home, and eventually get a scholarship to their college of choice, we may be inclined to take credit for a parenting job well done. If the primary means we use to that end are rewards and consequences, though, we can send our kids off with a "What's in it for me?" approach toward life choices.

When my daughter, LeeAnne, was three years old, she expressed the essence of the parental obedience challenge when she told my wife, Jane, "Mommy, I can't wanna do it!"

We're called to help our children "wanna do it" for the right reasons.

I do not get embarrassed by my children's behavior very easily. . . . I try to stay calm and deal with their behavior as privately as I can. I do not want to embarrass them. I usually try to whisper in their ear and, if needed, remove them to a more private location, so we can deal with the issue without an audience.

—Michelle, mother of five

I'd like to think that I am consistent, whether in public or not, but that's just not true. When my kids were younger and had shorter memories and attention spans, public discipline generally entailed finding a bathroom or quiet private place. Now that they're older, I generally wait and address the issue when we are at home.

—Diane, mother of two

The consequences and discipline are no different either in public or privately. If they were, it would be a double standard, and not what I want the kids to learn. Behavior at home is just as important as behavior out where people may see.

—Allison, mother of three

OBEYING LIKE JESUS

Leading like Jesus in our parenting always involves modeling and nurturing obedience. We're ordained by God as our children's primary instructors and models of what it means to be in an obedient relationship. We're responsible for their first impressions of obedience.

If we give obedience a bad name, it will carry far-reaching consequences. As one commentator put it, "If children resist obeying their parents, they are likely to resist and disobey others with authority in their lives and eventually consider disobeying God."

> *Then he went down to Nazareth with them and was*
> *obedient to them. . . . And Jesus grew in wisdom and stature,*
> *and in favor with God and men. (Luke 2:51-52)*

Obedience to His parents played a major role in preparing Jesus for His life's work.

He grew in wisdom, the ability to make the best choices reflecting what mattered most to God.

He grew in stature, the physical strength and skills needed to do the work set before Him.

He grew in the eyes of God, becoming more attuned to His Father as He progressed from infancy to manhood.

He grew in the eyes of men as the godliness of His character was expressed in how He treated other people and their trust and respect increased.

The fact that the word "obey" appears 165 times in the Bible—along with numerous references to obedience and submission—is a clear indication that obedience matters to God. In the life of Jesus, obedience holds the highest place as the expression of His loving relationship with His Father—the relationship He calls us to experience with Him. In fact, loving obedience is what Jesus proclaimed as the reason for all He did and said. It's what He held up as the key expression of a loving relationship with Him:

"If you love me, show it by doing what I've told you. . . .

"If anyone loves me, he will carefully keep my word and my Father will love him—we'll move right into the neighborhood! . . .

"But so the world might know how thoroughly I love the Father, I am carrying out my Father's instructions right down to the last detail. . . .

"If you keep my commands, you'll remain intimately at home in my love. That's what I've done—kept my Father's commands and made myself at home in his love." (John 14:15, 23, 31; 15:10, MSG)

It was in obedience that Jesus said, "My Father, if it is possible, may this cup be taken from me. Yet not as I will, but as you will" (Matthew 26:39). In obedience He went to the cross on our behalf. And Ephesians 6:1-3 offers a reward to children who obey and honor their parents: long lives that will "go well with" them.

With these things in mind, a prayer for our children and our parenting might go like this: "Lord, help us direct our children in the things that matter to You so that they will be equipped to fully live the life You have set before them in Your grace and mercy. We acknowledge we can't teach or model what we don't know; nor can we require obedience from our children if we're not willing to follow You. Help us to obey. Father, create in us an obedient heart so we may guide our children to You and to the life path You would have them follow."

It's a prayer I don't think we can pray enough.

HOW ARE YOU DOING?

Is your parenting likely to provoke disobedience? Take this quiz to find out. Answer "true" or "false" for each statement.

_____ I make obedience optional.

_____ I'm willing to negotiate lower standards of behavior to avoid a hassle.

____ I look the other way and ignore disobedience when it's too inconvenient to address.

____ I delay delivering appropriate consequences as well as praise.

____ I'm inconsistent in applying standards for acceptable behavior.

____ I model misbehavior, matching anger with anger.

____ I issue idle threats.

____ I'm inconsistent in my responses and in delivering promised consequences.

____ I demand perfection before recognizing progress.

____ I'm not sure my kids really understand what I require of them.

____ I overreact out of anger or frustration.

____ I've established too many rules.

____ I deliver too many variations in consequences between children.

____ I reward bad behavior by paying more attention to it.

The more "true" statements you found in this list, the more you risk inspiring rebellion instead of obedience. Inconsistency, weak or delayed follow-through, out-of-control rulemaking, and emotion-based discipline are among the most common encouragers of disobedience. If that's your situation, the following six tips for inspiring obedience may help.

TIP #1: STAND YOUR GROUND

One question you have to answer when guiding children toward obedience is this: Are you willing to invest the time and energy to withstand their challenges?

The following is a dialogue between my son-in-law, Paul, and his four-year-old son, John.

PAUL: "Johnny, come here." Paul points to a spot in front of him.

JOHN (*standing away from his dad*): "How about here?"

PAUL: "No. I said come *here*."

JOHN (*moving closer*): "How about *here?*"

PAUL (*pointing at an exact location*): "No, come *here.*"

JOHN (*with an impish grin, moving a short distance forward*): "How about *here?*"

The dialogue continues in this manner for another ten minutes, until John finally stands where his father had instructed him to stand.

Both father and son were making choices in this parental leadership moment. If only physical compliance had been at stake, Paul could have eliminated any further choices by exerting his authority and physical superiority, placing his son where he wanted him to be. Or he could have attempted to bribe John into doing what he was being asked to do. In that case, the lesson being taught would have been about power and control. The test of wills would have been quickly concluded until the next time John wanted to try his luck.

In this case, Paul chose to exercise patience and persistence to allow his son an opportunity for a change of heart that could grow into wanting to make the right choice.

Pause & Reflect

- What would you have done in Paul's place?
- Are there times you give in too easily because it takes too much effort to stand your ground?

TIP #2: DON'T LET FEAR SET YOUR AGENDA

Children are God's appointed training aides in the spiritual development of their parents. They test our patience, endurance, faith, priorities, compassion, and obedience in loving as we are loved. They have instant access to our vul-

nerabilities to pride and fear; they provide instant feedback on our performance. Nothing will get us on our knees before the Lord faster than our
children.

As parents, we are confronted daily with choices when we respond to the
emerging egos of our kids. If *no* isn't the first word an infant utters, it's a close
second—and *mine* isn't far behind. When our parenting is challenged, keeping
our own egos in check can be a daunting task.

Imagine a trip to the grocery store with your four-year-old. You're hurrying
to get a few things for dinner before picking up your older child at school. As
you proceed down a crowded aisle, your normally compliant child decides to
throw a temper tantrum when told that he can't keep the box of cookies he has
somehow managed to put in the basket.

Every conflict is an opportunity—for growth, for learning, for character
development. Every discipline moment needs to point my children right
back to their need of a savior and God's goodness in providing one! I'm
thankful for their repentance and I don't hesitate to make sure that they
know that their dad and I are praying for them.

—DIANE, mother of two

As his tantrum escalates, you notice the disapproving looks of shoppers
around you. You glance at your watch. You're running late; it's decision time.
How will you respond to your child? What fears would affect your choices at
this moment?

___ fear of embarrassment

___ fear of the opinion of others

___ fear of inadequacy

___ fear of losing control

___ other

What would your primary concern be during this public challenge of your parenting skills? If it's fear, remember truths like these from God's Word:

> *For God did not give us a spirit of timidity, but a spirit*
> *of power, of love and of self-discipline. (2 Timothy 1:7)*

> *And we know that in all things God works for the*
> *good of those who love him, who have been called*
> *according to his purpose. (Romans 8:28)*

> *I can do everything through him who gives*
> *me strength. (Philippians 4:13)*

TIP #3: TAILOR YOUR TACTICS

How would you deal with the aforementioned situation in the grocery store?

____ verbal threats

____ bribery

____ physical punishment

____ a quick exit

What lesson would you want your child to learn that would shape his behavior the next time?

When I asked my daughter, LeeAnne, now a mother of three, what she would do, she responded with a very wise answer: "It would depend on which child I was dealing with." Her three children have totally different personalities.

I was impressed with two aspects of her response. First, she—not her four-year-old—would control the moment. Second, she was prepared to adjust her approach to fit the development level and personality of the child. A strong word of disapproval might bring her daughter back in line, but physical removal from the store might be required to deal with her son.

It's important to discipline fairly, without playing favorites. When it comes to teaching obedience, though, one size rarely fits all. Failing to take our children's differences into account can exasperate them without educating them (Ephesians 6:4).

TIP #4: MODEL OBEDIENCE YOURSELF

To small children, parents are the image of God. How they see you is how they'll be inclined to see Him. How you treat them will either inspire willing obedience or willful resistance in their relationship with you—and ultimately with God. In other words, *what they see is what you get.*

It doesn't stop there, either. What kids learn from their parents, they're likely to pass on to their children.

It's instinctive for children to imitate their parents, especially the one of the same gender. Often kids don't distinguish between good or bad behavior. They're like sponges, absorbing everything they see parents say or do. For parents this is a big responsibility, because we know the most powerful training happens not when we say it, but when we live it.

It certainly works that way at my son Phil's house. There the word "stupid"—directed at another person and out of earshot of a parent—is often reported by a self-righteous sibling anxious to see what discipline the offender will receive. One day not long ago Phil was playing basketball while his son watched from the sidelines. In a moment of frustration after missing an easy basket, Phil mumbled, "Boy, that was a stupid shot."

After the game, Phil's son asked why he had used the "S" word and when it would be okay for him to use it, too. To his credit, Phil took the time to explain that, although he had not directed his remark to anyone, it still was not a good thing to say. He then asked his son whether he wanted to be someone who used words that could hurt people. His son replied, "No." Phil concluded the conversation by saying, "Neither do I."

There are times we see our faults most clearly when they're reflected by our children. Want to know your flaws? Wait and watch for them to crop up in your kids.

My grandkids love stories about how I was disciplined by my mom and dad for some familiar infraction like pestering my sister or getting caught trying to get out of going to school by playing sick. They like picturing me as a little kid and knowing that I made some of the mistakes they've made.

I'm amused to hear my grown-up kids express dismay that their children are struggling with the same issues that concerned them at the same age. Then they laugh at themselves and say, "I sound just like my parents." Yes, and I often sounded like my parents. The cycle, it seems, continues.

The same was true of Jesus' family. He had wonderful footsteps to follow. Before Jesus was born, Joseph and Mary proved themselves to be surrendered to the will of God in their lives:

> *"I am the Lord's servant," Mary answered. "May it be to me*
> *as you have said." Then the angel left her. (Luke 1:38)*

> *But after he had considered this, an angel of the Lord*
> *appeared to him in a dream and said, "Joseph son of*
> *David, do not be afraid to take Mary home as your wife,*
> *because what is conceived in her is from the Holy Spirit."* . . .
> *When Joseph woke up, he did what the angel*
> *of the Lord had commanded him and took Mary*
> *home as his wife. (Matthew 1:20, 24)*

Like Mary and Joseph, we can pass on a legacy of obedience. Charles Spurgeon put it this way: "As parents, we wish so to live that our children may copy us to their lasting profit."

What matters is whether the cycle is one of positive or negative role-modeling. What I modeled as a parent is now being acted out by my grandchildren's mothers and fathers. Seeing that, I thank God for His guidance and grace. I'm awed that the "lasting profit" Spurgeon talked about can be for generations we'll never see this side of heaven.

TIP #5: BUILD TRUST

The Living Bible paraphrases Ephesians 6:4 this way: "And now a word to you parents. Don't keep on scolding and nagging your children, making them angry and resentful. Rather, bring them up with loving discipline the Lord himself approves, with suggestions and godly advice."

How can parents inspire obedience instead of provoking anger and resentment? Part of the answer lies in trust.

Trust is required for willing obedience. In their early lives, our children assume us trustworthy until proven otherwise. As they grow in their ability to make choices, the temptation to test the boundaries of our rules and resolve frequently proves irresistible. To guide children toward obedience, we must respond to their challenges without eroding trust—moving them closer to obedience and away from rebellion.

How can you nurture obedience by building trust in your children? Here are nine ways:

- Establish a limited number of reasonable, age-appropriate rules and boundaries.
- Explain the reason why you're setting those limits, especially with older children.
- Praise progress.
- Praise early confession of wrongdoing.
- Deliver praise and consequences in a timely, specific manner.
- Compliment obedience.
- Make every response a loving response.
- Admit when you've made a mistake.
- Apologize when appropriate.

TIP #6: TEST FOR UNDERSTANDING

If you want your child to obey, it's vital to provide clear direction and information in a loving way.

Be specific about what you expect. Describe what a good job looks like in terms your children understand. If your instructions are too general or too complicated, the likelihood of frustration and discouragement increases. "Be nice to your sister" can be mistranslated into anything from painting a sibling blue to offering her a second chew on one's gum.

Define your terms, too. Several years ago my daughter heard my granddaughter crying in the family room, where she'd been playing with her favorite red ball. As my daughter went to investigate, she encountered her young son exiting the room carrying the ball. She asked him why his sister was crying and why he had her ball. With his chin in the air he replied, "I'm sharing!"

I am not a perfect mom, so I do make mistakes. There are some things I do that I hope my kids won't, but I know that Jesus has faith that I can raise my children right. He is definitely leading me. There's no better satisfaction than to hear words of praise from your children's lips of the one and true God.

—DANIELLE, mother of two

One of the easiest ways to nurture obedience is ensuring that the concepts involved are understood. Testing for understanding is the key to avoiding frustration.

It's not enough to be clear, though. In the words of Ephesians 4:15, "speaking the truth in love" is our goal. To follow the example of Jesus as a leader, never make children feel inferior because of a failure on their part. As Jesus did, let the love you have for your children come through.

HIGH HOPES, HIGH CALLING

What's your highest hope for your children? Does it include living well and having a long life, growing in wisdom, stature, and in the eyes of God and men, developing a love relationship with Jesus Christ, and fulfilling the purpose God has for their lives? If it does, you'll want them to know and practice the true meaning of the word *obey*.

To help your children attain all you hope for them, show them the benefits of obedience. The level and consistency of your trust in and obedience to God will pour blessings into their lives.

Leadership is about going somewhere. It's about making a difference. When you lead your family like Jesus, the difference you hope to make is that your children will not only obey you, but also obey God—and be a beneficial part of His family as well as yours.

I need to stop reacting emotionally to my children's struggles. I teach in our children's ministry at church and at one time had my own son in my class. As I had to correct a group of boys for getting a little wild, I noticed that I could do it calmly and without any irritation unless my son was in the group. When my son was involved, I got aggravated and tended to be harsher sounding. I became emotionally involved and I reacted based on emotion.

—MICHELLE, mother of five

Pause & Reflect

- Which two of the following were your parents best at? Which two did they have the most trouble with? Which two are easiest for you? Hardest? Which two do you think your children will need most from you during the coming year?

  ___ standing your ground

  ___ not letting fear set your agenda

  ___ tailoring your tactics

  ___ modeling obedience yourself

  ___ building trust

  ___ testing for understanding

- Which of the following do you think would help most as you work on developing the skills and qualities you just identified?

  ___ your spouse's support

  ___ prayer

  ___ reading this book again

  ___ finding a mentor

  ___ other

Points to Ponder about the *Hands* of Leading Like Jesus as a Parent

- There are two parts to the servant leadership that Jesus exemplified:
    1. A visionary role—setting the course and the destination
    2. An implementation role—doing things right with a focus on serving

- A key activity of an effective servant parent is to act as a performance coach—making an ongoing investment in the lives of your children.

- There are three parts of being a servant parent: performance planning, day-to-day coaching, and performance evaluation. A family leader's main focus should be on day-to-day coaching—helping your children accomplish agreed-upon goals. This is where the traditional pyramid hierarchy must be turned upside-down.

- Parents can coach kids through the four stages of learning a new task or skill: Novice (just starting out); Apprentice(in training); Journeyman (capable of working on his or her own); Master teacher (highly skilled and able to teach others).

- The role of a parent is the same throughout the transformation process—to provide what your children need to advance to the next stage.

- Your ultimate goal as a parent is to model obedience to God for your children so that they can enjoy His many blessings.

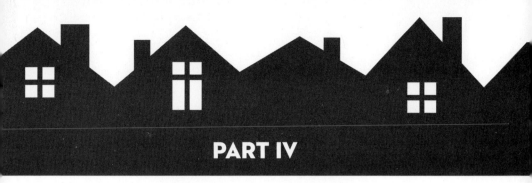

PART IV

THE HABITS

As a leader committed to serve despite all the pressures, trials, and temptations He faced, how did Jesus replenish His energy and servant perspective? Through His habits!

Your habits are the way you review and act on your daily commitment as a parent to serve rather than being served. In this section Ken highlights five key habits Jesus applied to stay on track with His mission, and shows how these habits can help you parent like Jesus. Next, Tricia emphasizes—from a parenting perspective—three of those habits: spending time in solitude, prayer, and relying on the Word of God. Phil concludes by sharing what might be the greatest of all parenting habits: forgiveness and grace.

TEN

Time with God—
A Dad's Perspective

PRINCIPLE 10

To Lead Like Jesus, Stay on Track by Staying Close to Him

The responsibilities, distractions, and occasional conflicts of family life can pull any well-meaning parent off track. In this chapter Ken explores five powerful habits that can help you stick with leading your family as Jesus would.

When announcing emergency procedures before an airplane takes off, the flight attendant always instructs parents to put on their oxygen masks before giving oxygen to their children. Why? Because unless the parent is breathing, the kids won't have a good chance of breathing, either.

In the same way, it's important for family leaders to "breathe in" God's love and wisdom first—so that they can transmit His blessings to their kids.

What gets you up in the morning? If you're like most of us, your alarm clock goes off. Think about that term, "alarm." I once heard my friend, pastor John Ortberg, wonder, "Why isn't it the 'opportunity' clock? Or the 'it's going to be a great day' clock? No, it's the *alarm* clock!"

So, the alarm goes off. You leap out of bed and you're into your task-oriented self. You're trying to eat while you're washing and you're checking your e-mail as you get dressed.

If you're like a lot of people, you jump in the car. Maybe you're on the phone while you're driving. Next, you're going to this meeting and that meeting and running from here to there.

Finally, you get home at eight or nine at night. You're absolutely exhausted, so when you fall into bed you don't even have energy to say goodnight to your spouse who might be lying next to you.

Next morning—*bang!*—the alarm goes off and you're at it again.

Pretty soon you're in a rat race. As Hollywood philosopher Lily Tomlin once said, "The problem with a rat race is that even if you win it, you're still a rat."

I think too often as parents we're caught in an activity rat race. What we have to do is find a way to enter our day slowly, so we can awaken our thoughtful, reflective self first.

For example, for years my friend and coauthor Jim Ballard went jogging every morning. People would ask him, "How far do you go?"

Jim would reply, "I don't know."

Then they'd ask, "How long do you run?"

"I don't know," he'd say. "My running isn't about getting anywhere. It's the way I choose to enter my day."

How we do that makes a difference. Every morning when we wake up, the Evil One—also known as the devil—is waiting to hook our false pride or fear and focus our energy on self-serving interests. To be parents who lead like Jesus, we need to resist this temptation and renew our daily commitment to stay on track and serve rather than be served.

As Jesus moved through His season of earthly leadership, He was often tempted to go off course. He was continually pressured to respond to the failings of His friends and enemies. Yet He stayed on track with His mission by practicing the following five key habits that countered the negative forces arrayed against Him.

THE FIRST HABIT: SOLITUDE

In our Lead Like Jesus Encounter workshops, we ask participants to take forty-five minutes of solitude—a time when they don't talk to anyone, use their computers or cell phones, or have any other distractions.

We ask them to begin by putting their hands, palms down, on their knees and thinking of anything they're concerned about. As a concern appears in their mind, they mentally put it down at the foot of the cross. When they have completed thinking about their concerns, they turn their hands upward in a posture of receiving, contemplating some aspect of the character of God—such as His mercy, love, grace, or power. We encourage them to listen without any agenda.

Before we send people off for their period of solitude, we have them recite Psalm 46:10 with us in this way:

> *Be still and know that I am God.*
> *Be still and know.*
> *Be still.*
> *Be.*

When people return from their solitude, they have big smiles on their faces. While many of them find it difficult to quiet their minds, they say it was a powerful experience.

The reality is that most of us spend little, if any, time in solitude. Yet if we don't, how can God have a chance to talk with us?

Pause & Reflect

- Try the solitude exercise used in our workshop. Then tell your spouse or a friend what happened.
- How would your day be different if you did the other things I've just described?

I love to start my day with solitude. When I'm on top of my game, I sit at the side of the bed and recite something I learned from Henry Blackaby:

> *Good morning, Daddy! What are You up to today?*
> *How can I help? I'm available.*

Then I just sit and listen, to see if the good Lord has something for me to do that day. I'm amazed at some of the wonderful thoughts I receive.

If nothing comes, I recite the following:

> *Lord, clear me out of me. Fill me up with You*
> *and then clothe me with humility.*

Then I listen again.

If I don't take time when I first wake up, I take some quiet time when I get in the car. I used to automatically turn the radio on, but now I use the fifteen minutes it takes me to get to our office to quiet myself and see if anything becomes clear to me.

A friend of ours told Phil and me how she decides whether something that comes to her is from the Lord. She has a two-step test. The first is, "Could I have thought of this myself?" If the answer is no, the next question is: "Would the devil like me to do it?" If the answer to that question is also no, she knows she's on to something.

Phil has a wonderful saying that I also like to quote in the morning:

> *In the morning I rest my arms awhile on*
> *the windowsill of heaven and gaze upon the face*
> *of the Lord. Then, with that vision in mind,*
> *I turn strong and meet the day.*

A good practice is to get up in the morning and observe some quiet time. Why? Because solitude is being completely alone with God without an agenda. As Henri Nouwen wrote in *Life of the Beloved*, "Solitude is taking time to listen for the 'small, still voice' through which God speaks to your soul and tells you that *you are the Beloved.*" When we don't take time for solitude, we jump right away into our task-oriented selves and fill our time with trivial tasks that fail to enrich our spirits.

Jesus modeled solitude as an integral, strategic component of His leadership. My favorite example of this comes from the book of Mark, where Jesus had to make a tough choice between a *good* use of His time and the *best* use of His time.

> That evening, after the sun was down, they brought sick and evil-afflicted people to him, the whole city lined up at his door! He cured their sick bodies and tormented spirits. Because the demons knew his true identity, he didn't let them say a word.
>
> While it was still night, way before dawn, he got up and went out to a secluded spot and prayed. Simon and those with him went looking for him. They found him and said, "Everybody's looking for you."
>
> Jesus said, "Let's go to the rest of the villages so I can preach there also. This is why I've come." (Mark 1:32-38, MSG)

"While it was still night, way before dawn, he got up and went out to a secluded spot and prayed." These words stand between Jesus and the temptation to spend His precious time doing the good and popular thing instead of doing the primary work for which He had come.

Imagine Jesus' intense compassion for the sick and demon-possessed people He would have to leave. Imagine how strong the temptation would have been for Him to stay and use His healing powers to the delight of all. His disciples expected Jesus to seize this opportunity because He was the Messiah who would call Israel to God. But they thought like men, and Jesus had just heard from His Father.

What allowed Jesus to resist doing this *good* work and pick the *best*? In solitude and prayer, away from the hopes and hurts of those who looked to Him with high and compelling expectations, Jesus again received instructions on the best use of the next day from the Father.

Pause & Reflect

- What's an example of *best* parenting work that might replace *good* parenting work?
- Have you ever gotten away with God in prayer and solitude to resist doing good work and instead discovered the best work? What happened?

THE SECOND HABIT: PRAYER

As Jesus demonstrated, prayer and solitude often go together. Prayer isn't just a wish list; it's a way to quiet yourself and commune with the Lord. As Jesus prayed,

> *"Our Father in heaven, hallowed be your name,*
> *your kingdom come, your will be done on earth*
> *as it is in heaven." (Matthew 6:9-10, emphasis added)*

Prayer is really a way to find out what His will is for you—in parenting and every other area.

When that time of honest reflection reveals a problem to be faced, prayer is also the most powerful first step to bringing God's promises into the equation. As we've mentioned before, this one can be especially encouraging to a family leader:

> *Do not be anxious about anything, but in everything,*
> *by prayer and petition, with thanksgiving, present your*
> *requests to God. And the peace of God, which transcends all*
> *understanding, will guard your hearts and your minds in*
> *Christ Jesus. (Philippians 4:6-7)*

People ask me all the time how to pray. While I'm not an expert, let me share what I've learned. First, prayer is not a technique; it's essentially a conversation with God. We all need to develop our own style of conversing with the Father. If you'd like a framework to get started, let me suggest ACTS as a way to begin. I learned this from my friend Bob Buford, author of *Halftime*. This simple acronym—ACTS—can help you remember the four basic parts of prayer. It has helped many beginners and served as a compass for weather-beaten veterans. Try it for a few days.

A is for adoration. All prayer should begin here. Tell the Lord that you love Him and appreciate Him for who He is.

> *Yours, O LORD, is the greatness and the power and*
> *the glory and the majesty and the splendor, for*
> *everything in heaven and earth is yours.*
> *Yours, O LORD, is the kingdom; you are exalted*
> *as head over all. (1 Chronicles 29:11)*

C is for confession. When we come into the presence of a holy God, we immediately sense our inadequacies and are convicted that we all fall short of God's glory. Our response is confession. What did you do yesterday as a family leader that you wish you hadn't? Sometimes we have to confess our transgressions even before we express our adoration and love.

> *If we confess our sins, he is faithful and just*
> *and will forgive us our sins and purify us from*
> *all unrighteousness. (1 John 1:9)*

T is for thanksgiving. Thanksgiving is the heartfelt expression of gratitude to God for all He has done in creation, in redemption, and in our lives. During this part of the prayer, thank God specifically for all He's done for you since the last time you talked. As the old hymn says, "Count your blessings, name them one by one. Count your many blessings; see what God has done." What are you particularly thankful for as a parent? And what if tomorrow you had only the things you thanked God for today?

Sing and make music in your heart to the Lord, always giving
thanks to God the Father for everything, in the name
of our Lord Jesus Christ. (Ephesians 5:19-20)

S is for supplication. Finally, we get to the part of prayer where most of us start—asking. Supplication is just a big word for asking for what you need. Start by praying about the needs of others, including family members; then ask for your own needs to be met. It's okay to have a big wish list. According to God's Word, we can ask with confidence:

Ask and it will be given to you; seek and you will find; knock
and the door will be opened to you. (Matthew 7:7)

Pause & Reflect

- One of the most revealing questions you can ask a parent is, "How is your prayer life?" The answer will speak volumes about where and how that parent is leading his or her family. How would you answer that question?
- How would you *like* to answer it?

My prayer life is about constant communication with Jesus. I don't have a prayer closet, but I pray in the car, at my desk, while I'm cleaning or doing laundry, or wherever He brings something to my heart. I talk to Him, and then listen to what He wants to tell my heart. What I hear is weighed by Scripture, and then acted upon if necessary.

—ALLISON, mother of three

Prayer life is a personal thing. I used to think that my prayer life was horrible. After all, I am a busy working mom of five. I simply didn't have time to sit down and have a quiet time with God. The only time my house is quiet is the middle of the night, and on the rare occasion that I get to sit and be still, I usually end up falling asleep. But I realized that I am speaking with God throughout my day. Scripture tells us to pray continually. While I don't have a quiet time, I do spend my day with God in many ways.

—MICHELLE, mother of five

THE THIRD HABIT: STUDYING AND APPLYING SCRIPTURE

Margie and I have fun supporting each other in our study of the Bible. Every morning we read a devotional my mother started giving me when I was ten years old. We also read Sarah Young's *Jesus Calling*, that offers daily, Bible-based insights about staying attuned to the Lord. I participate in a men's Bible study group on the phone; Margie talks once a week with the wives of those men. As couples, we meet at least once a year with our Bible teacher, Richard Case. Margie keeps affirmations and Bible quotes on her night table.

Every day I read or recite some of my favorite Bible quotes. For example, we have a psalm taped on the mirror in our bathroom. It helps us start the day off with a positive attitude.

> *This is the day the LORD has made;*
> *let us rejoice and be glad in it. (Psalm 118:24)*

Sadly, when our kids were very young, they missed growing up in a household where we were reading and studying Scripture. When Scott and Debbie were just two and three years old, Margie and I became very annoyed when our pastor was fired—unjustly, we felt—by the congregation. We said, "If that's what Christianity is all about, they can have it." We turned our backs on the church, except for attending Easter and Christmas Eve services. If you'd asked our kids at age eighteen to recite the Lord's Prayer, they probably couldn't have done it.

Our kids are on their own spiritual journeys now. Margie and I do our best to love on them and set good examples. I kiddingly tell Scott and Debbie that I didn't sign up for the Lord until I was forty-eight, so they have a few years until they get there—but if they hit forty-eight and they're not on the Lord's team, I'm coming after them!

We also spend time with our three grandsons—Alec, Kyle, and Kurtis—to help them on their spiritual journeys. At every family meal we have, they always ask me to lead the blessing. I also gave the older grandkids a copy of my spiritual journey, titled *It Takes Less Than a Minute to Suit Up for the Lord.*

Scripture has become an important part of our lives. We hope and pray that it will become important to our kids' and grandkids' lives as well, because there's so much wisdom in the Bible.

Pause & Reflect

- **Where are you with studying and applying the Bible? Which stage of my family's journey in this area do you identify with most?**
- **What are you doing to help your kids realize that the Bible is the greatest book of all time?**

There is a Bible verse I've memorized and turn to it daily. It's Philippians 4:11-12 (NASB): "Not that I speak from want, for I have learned to be content in whatever circumstances I am. I know how to get along with humble means, and I also know how to live in prosperity; in any and every circumstance I have learned the secret of being filled and going hungry, both of having abundance and suffering need." Once that comes to mind, the pressures of the moment tend to fade away.

—ALLISON, mother of three

*Each day we make a commitment to read our Bible together as a family—
usually first thing in the morning. At the end of the day we share or listen to
other family members share where or what we think God has taught us
today. It's one day at a time and we try to hold each other accountable,
asking, "Did you read God's Word today? What did you read? Did you
hear God's voice? What did He say to you?"*

—JENNIFER, mother of two

*Opa, my grandfather, says not to confuse quantity with quality. I try to
find a verse that speaks to me and think over it for several days. When I'm
worried or happy or stressed or sad, I'll think about it. This meditation
keeps God's Word close. I don't have the hours that I used to have to spend
in God's Word, but I still find that He works through me.*

—AMY, mother of four

THE FOURTH HABIT: ACCEPTING GOD'S UNCONDITIONAL LOVE

Jesus stayed close to His Father by constantly trusting His Father's unconditional love, even to the end. To me, this verse explains why:

> *"For I know the plans I have for you," declares the Lord,
> "plans to prosper you and not to harm you, plans to give you
> hope and a future." (Jeremiah 29:11)*

It's hard to accept God's love when you don't have a good model of what
unconditional love looks like. Not all of us have had a positive relationship with
our earthly fathers and mothers to bring into our own parenting.

In our Leadership Encounter workshops we have an exercise in which we ask
people to think of something they wish their parents or other important adults
had said to them when they were young—something that would have made
them feel better about themselves. It could be as simple as "I love you." Half the
group sits in a circle and half the group stands behind those who are seated.

When we say "go," the people standing lean down and whisper to those sitting in front of them the supportive words they wish they'd heard as children. Then they move to the person to their right and whisper the same words to him or her. They continue doing this until they've completed going around the circle, so that every participant gets to share his or her love statement a number of times.

Then people reverse roles, so that those standing now sit and hear a variety of love statements. Encounter attendees tell us this is one of the most healing exercises they've ever participated in, particularly when we do a second round and give everybody a "love" Bible quote. Here are two examples:

> *"My command is this: Love each other*
> *as I have loved you." (John 15:12)*

> *No one has ever seen God; but if we love one another, God lives in*
> *us and his love is made complete in us. (1 John 4:12)*

When it comes to staying close to God, accepting His unconditional love and transferring it to others is a powerful habit.

Unfortunately, I see a lot of parents whose love—because they're mere mortals—is conditional. When their kids make a mistake, the parents seem to repossess their acceptance and affection. Margie and I always tried to separate our love from our kids' behavior; they always had our love. We might not like their behavior, but love wasn't something they had to earn. It was a given.

Pause & Reflect

- Think of a time when you experienced God's love for you in a specific way, the true significance of which only He and you knew. How did you feel?
- Were you able to transfer that good feeling to others in your family? Why or why not?

THE FIFTH HABIT: INVOLVEMENT IN
SUPPORTIVE RELATIONSHIPS

Staying close to God is tougher when you try to live the Christian life alone. That's why the fifth habit is vitally important to you—and your family.

An accountability group can provide the support you need. Who in your life is willing to pat you on the back when you're "on your game" and be honest with you when you're off track? Candid feedback can be invaluable to your spiritual growth. Jesus had a small, intimate group—John, James, and Peter—with whom He could be vulnerable.

One of the values Margie and I have passed on to our kids is the importance of sustaining supportive relationships over a long period of time. Old friends have a lot of deposits in your interpersonal bank. They usually tell you the truth because they can draw from that account.

It's wise to schedule supportive relationships into your calendar. I'm in a men's support group and Margie is in one for women. We've been in these groups for a number of years, getting together every four to six weeks to help each other lead the kind of lives we want to lead. Our son, Scott, is in a men's support group that meets monthly. Debbie has an unofficial but close group of friends who are there to support each other.

Families often need accountability, too. Our company, for instance, is run by Margie and me, Margie's brother Tom, and Scott and Debbie. When our kids and Tom decided they wanted to join our company almost twenty years ago, we formed a family council and hired an outside consultant to work with us. For the better part of fifteen years, that consultant has met with us one day every quarter so that conflicts don't fester. Everybody gets a chance to share what's happening and resolve any issues.

You may not be able to hire a consultant, but a pastor or counselor might help. Your family is too important to let resentments go unhealed. Spending face-to-face time with your accountability group and other supportive people in your life can keep you and your family on track—and closer to God.

Pause & Reflect

- Name two special people in your life who love you enough to tell you what you need to hear about your parenting. How are you improving as a result of those relationships?
- What can you do this week to make sure your supportive relationships stay alive and well?
- What fellow parent needs you to hold him or her accountable? Do you love that person enough to say what he or she needs to hear?

I'm very blessed to have extremely close friends—and my hubby—who are "tell it like it is" people. We get together regularly to talk about the deep issues, not just surface concerns, and hold each other's feet to the Scriptures.

—ALLISON, mother of three

The accountability of my Tuesday morning Bible study group has been life-changing. The women in this group are constantly praying for each other, encouraging each other, and brainstorming [solutions to] difficult family situations. The best part about it is that nurturing these relationships has meant spending lots of time together. We have cookouts with our husbands and kids and girls' night dinners without them!

—ROBIN, mother of three

My husband is the best at telling me the cold, hard truth gently and in love—most of the time! We invest a lot of time in our relationship and hold each other accountable when we need to. I have one or two close friends who don't hesitate to point things out to me, and vice versa. It's difficult to find that time to spend together, but we do what we can.

—Diane, mother of two

ELEVEN

Time with God— A Mom's Perspective

PRINCIPLE 11
To Lead Like Jesus, Meet Challenges by Meeting with Him

Moms and Dads who want to be family leaders need to stay connected with their heavenly Father. In this chapter Tricia shows how time alone, communicating with God, is one of the most powerful, accessible, and useful resources for coping with— and triumphing over—the challenges that parenting can bring.

The other day one of my single friends posted this statement on Facebook: "I love listening to silence."

My response: "I've heard of that before."

As a mom of four children ranging in age from two to twenty-three, I can testify that our house never seems empty. Never. I can't remember the last time I've been the only one home and really experienced silence. Even as I type this I can hear three voices talking over each other in an adjoining room.

Yet there is a time when I experience a sense of quiet. It comes at six o'clock in the morning, while everyone else in the house is still sleeping. I slip out of bed and tiptoe to the kitchen. Once I get a pot of coffee going I pull out my Bible, Bible study pages, and a journal. With the sounds of snores coming from the bedrooms I read God's Word.

I write down Scripture passages. In my journal, I also share what's on my heart. There I write down my frustrations, worries, and praises—and turn it all over to God.

By the time I hear my husband getting into the shower or my toddler calling "Mama" from her crib, I feel more prepared for the day. Meeting God first reminds me that He is in control. There is nothing I will face that day that will come as a surprise to Him.

As for Bible reading, I can't tell you how many times I've read a Scripture passage that's helped me later that very day. It's like getting a pep talk from a coach before you head into the football game. Our coach, Jesus, knows exactly which "plays" to run and the obstacles we'll face. He loves to prepare us ahead of time, if we'll let Him.

TRUE CONFESSIONS

There are two things I have to confess, though. First, I haven't always valued time spent with God. When I was first married with kids, sometimes days would pass without me really thinking about Him. Just as I had to create the habit of exercising and drinking enough water, I had to plan for time with Jesus, my Living Water. I knew if I didn't figure out a way to set aside time, it wasn't going to happen.

My planning started when I had a toddler and baby at home. I also babysat for a friend. Because I was caring for little kids all day, I set my alarm clock to get up fifteen minutes early. I was afraid the alarm would wake the baby, but it didn't. I can still remember Scripture verses God spoke to my heart and some of the prayers I prayed for my kids during those early morning hours—prayers I've seen answered in the last twenty years.

It was only fifteen minutes less sleep, but it did more to help my day than anything else. I became more caring and loving to my family. The little things that used to stress me out didn't seem as overwhelming. I was also able to find hope and encouragement to share with other moms. As I turned to Jesus, He helped me look beyond my own problems and to reach out to others with a compassionate heart.

My second confession is that this quiet time doesn't happen every day. (I, ahem, don't exercise every day either, though I try!) With a toddler in the house, there are times when she wakes up before I get a chance to slip away. There are also days when I've gotten on my computer to "just send one e-mail" and I've wasted my quiet time on messages or Facebook.

I can tell when that happens. Something just feels "off" for the rest of the day. My family can tell, too. I'm not as joyful or peaceful about, well, anything.

The power of solitude, prayer, and the study of Scripture can't be overemphasized. Together they can help us become parents who, like Jesus, are servant leaders.

Yet, as is so often the case, the things that benefit us most are usually the hardest to do.

GIVE YOURSELF A TIME-OUT

Of the five habits, *solitude* is by far the most elusive in our world of busyness and 24/7 communication. At any moment of the day—thanks to my computer and smartphone—people can reach me through phone call, Skype, e-mail, texting, Twitter, and Facebook!

Solitude is countercultural and challenging. It draws us into the very place from which so many of our efforts are designed to help us escape—being truly alone with God without an agenda.

For years my favorite scripture was the same one Ken mentioned in the previous chapter, Psalm 46:10: "Be still, and know that I am God." I'd recite that verse over and over to remind myself that life wasn't all about what I did, but also about allowing God to work in my stillness in ways only He could.

I also like the *New American Standard Bible* version of this verse: "Cease *striving* and know that I am God; I will be exalted among the nations, I will be exalted in the earth."

Sometimes the striving comes when things are going well and we don't want to get out of the flow. Sometimes it comes when we see that the people and things in our lives need attention. We roll up our sleeves and dig in.

Often it doesn't seem to make sense to stop what we're doing and turn to God by reading His Word and praying. Yet once you get a few minutes of peace, quiet, and *connection,* everything changes. It's like stepping out the back door of your noisy life of to-do lists and demanding relationships to breathe some fresh air.

When did you last spend significant time in solitude on purpose without a to-do, think, or prayer list and sat quietly in God's presence, listening to His "still small voice" (1 Kings 19:12, KJV)? If you can't remember, you now have a clue why your parenting may seem so hindered and unsatisfying. If you can remember and it was more than a week ago, you need to update your plans for the immediate future.

SOLITUDE PREPARES

Ken described earlier how Jesus showed that solitude was sometimes the best use of His time. He could have spent those hours healing and teaching, but the connection and solitude with His Father was even more important.

Solitude not only connects us with God, it also leads us to prepare for whatever's in store for our families. It helps us deal with the worries of the moment. It was in these times of preparing to lead, making important decisions, handling bad news, and dealing with praise and recognition that Jesus displayed for us the value of spending time alone to reset our spiritual compasses to find the "true north" of God's will and pleasure.

When preparing for the tests of leadership and public ministry, Jesus spent forty days alone in the desert (Matthew 4:1-11). How's that for some alone time? When Jesus was tested by Satan, He might have been hungry but through His solitude He clearly knew "who He was" and "whose He was." Satan didn't have a chance.

Before Jesus chose twelve apostles from among His followers, He spent the entire night alone in the desert hills (Luke 6:12-13). How often do you spend time alone to think and listen before making a major parenting decision?

When Jesus received the news of the death of John the Baptist, He withdrew in a boat to a solitary place (Matthew 14:13). Time alone can often help heal grief.

After the miraculous feeding of the five thousand, Jesus went up in the hills by Himself (Matthew 14:22-23). Since accolades follow great performance, solitude helps keep those rave reviews in perspective so that EGO doesn't take over.

Spending time with God not only gives us peace and prepares us for the day, it also allows Him to guide us in making decisions about our lives, our families, and our service. The most powerful example of the critical role that solitude played in the life and leadership of Jesus is described in the book of John, where Jesus was faced with a difficult choice of how best to use His time. Here's how the Bible describes the situation:

> *The people realized that God was at work among them in what*
> *Jesus had just done. They said, "This is the Prophet for sure,*
> *God's Prophet right here in Galilee!" Jesus saw that in their*
> *enthusiasm, they were about to grab him and make him king, so*
> *he slipped off and went back up the mountain to be by himself.*
> *(John 6:14-15, MSG)*

As Phil and Ken discussed earlier, our egos want to Edge God Out. Ego drives the self-interest that puffs us up inside. Ego tells us we are the head of the family and everyone just needs to listen to us and do what we say. Ego pushes our ideas, our agenda, and our comfort.

If anyone had a reason to have an ego it was Jesus. He could heal a sick man, calm a storm, turn water to wine, and raise a dead man to life. He could have told Himself, "I deserve to be made king. I deserve their praise. I should be rewarded for all I am and all I can do." But He didn't, did He?

Instead, Jesus humbled Himself, went away to a quiet place, and refocused

His mind and heart on His real purpose. What was that purpose? To model all that the law and prophets had to say about Him—and to die, providing the ultimate sacrifice for the people He loved so that we could spend eternity with God. As God-in-the flesh, He was to display His Father's love in a walking, breathing, loving, dying human body.

To know that Jesus was tempted to accept people's praise encourages me. I'm not the only one who faces the problem with wanting to be seen as a good parent. While I work hard in this area for the sake of my kids—and out of service to God—a part of me, if I'm honest, likes to get gold stars when my kids' positive behavior is noted by others.

The more each of us spends time with God, the better we are at determining His will for our families. We make better decisions as parents and have more success in our parenting. But with success comes another challenge: letting our egos inflate once again, instead of turning our eyes and our praise to God. The trouble comes when we pat ourselves on the back for the good job we're doing, or when we feel entitled to the praise of others, and once again Edge God Out.

I have made room for God in my schedule. As a mom it's hard to find time to be with God, but I've learned to steal snatches of time with Him when I can. When I first wake up I take time to pray about my day and for people I'm concerned about. I read the Bible for a few minutes while I'm eating my cereal. I put my laptop by the treadmill and watch an online sermon while I walk. I leave my Bible study workbook open on the table, and every time I walk by I read and answer a question before going on with household chores. I want to enjoy the presence of God all day long.

—CHRISTY, mother of two

In this toddler era, any solitude time seems near impossible! But perhaps what I should focus on is solitude in my mind. Even with noise—joyful

noise most of the time!—toddlers, and babies around me, I can take a few
minutes or even seconds to quiet my mind of the to-do lists, to just pray my
heart to Him. Or I can take one joy right there in the moment—my son's
blue eyes sparkling at me, for example—to praise and pray right then and
there.

—CAROLINE, mother of two

THE POWER OF PRAYER

Nobody seems to know who said this, but it's worth listening to: "One should never initiate anything that he cannot saturate with prayer." This couldn't be more true when it comes to parenting and becoming servant leaders in our homes.

If solitude is the most elusive of the habits for us to develop, *prayer* is the one that requires the most unlearning of old habits. Our prayer practices tend to be based on the traditions we grew up with, whether or not they help us and our families grow closer to God.

In my case, my mother dedicated her life to the Lord when I was in third grade; my stepfather was not a believer. Prayer, to our family, consisted of the few sentences we said at dinnertime: "Dear God, thank You for this food and all You've done for us. Amen."

When I attended church, I learned that the best time to pass notes to my friends was during prayer because no one was looking. I saw people prayed over when they were sick, and witnessed people turning to God in prayer when they had a problem.

But then I became a mom. That's when I learned that prayer is a conversation that can take place all day long. Yes, we can pray during those quiet morning hours—but we also can pray in the carpool lane or as we pile items into our grocery cart.

Prayer is an essential act of the will that demonstrates whether we're really serious about living and leading our families like Jesus. Without it we'll never be able to connect our plans and efforts with God's plan for His kingdom, or engage the spiritual resources Jesus promised in the work of the Holy Spirit. Seeking God's will through prayer, waiting in faith for an answer, acting in accordance with that answer, and being at peace with the outcome call for a level of spiritual maturity that will keep any parent seeking to lead like Jesus in the posture of a lifelong learner. The nature and objects of our prayers will determine whether we're EGO (Edging God Out)-driven or are glorifying our heavenly Father.

Pause & Reflect

- What did you learn about prayer as a child? Has it helped or hindered your prayer life as a parent?
- Have you ever asked someone to pray for you as a parent? If not, why not? If so, what was the result?

PRAYER REMINDS US WHO TO PRAISE

As parents, we'll never have the same type of success we might have in business. We won't get a promotion, and our story probably won't be written up in the Sunday paper. Yet there are other parents watching us, and some may congratulate us when our kids are kind and caring. Every small acknowledgement can be intoxicating to a parent, especially if we've bought into the formula we've mentioned before:

Self-worth = Performance + The Opinion of Others

I struggled with this for many years. My son Cory was born when I was seventeen, just three weeks after my high school graduation. When he was two months old I started college, determined to make something of myself. Part of my determination was based on wanting to be a good mom and role model for my son, but deep down I wanted to prove myself to others. I thought becoming a success would prove my worth.

While other moms were at the park with their kids, I was home writing articles and seeking publication. While other moms volunteered once a month to help in the nursery, I'd fill in whenever I was needed, even if it meant I often missed the worship service. While other moms read to their kids for fifteen minutes a day, I read to mine for an hour.

I wanted to be seen as a success in my career and in my volunteering, as well as in my parenting. That meant having the most perfect kids possible. I did get praise often, but not enough for my ego. Because of that, I wanted to do more and more.

We can hide a lot of things from a lot of people. But it's impossible to hide our true motivations and intentions from God. His Word reminds me that He was the source of any success I had. Listening to Him as I sat in silence, I would be reminded that He deserved my praise.

Taking time alone with God, your audience of One, is an important habit that will keep EGO from compromising your parenting. Handling compliments is serious business, as the Bible points out:

> *The crucible for silver and the furnace for gold, but man*
> *is tested by the praise he receives. (Proverbs 27:21)*

When you're seeking to parent as Jesus would, prayer should never be relegated to the status of last resort in times of deep distress. It's our most powerful, immediately accessible, and useful resource for responding to moment-to-moment family challenges.

Have a few minutes of time on your hands? Pray.

Don't have a minute to spare? Pray.

Feeling sad and overwhelmed? Pray.

Feeling excited about your family's future? Pray and thank God.

GOD proves to be good to the man who passionately waits, to the woman who diligently seeks. It's a good thing to quietly hope, quietly hope for help from GOD. It's a good thing when you're young to stick it out through the hard times. When life is heavy and hard to take, go off by yourself. Enter the silence. Bow in prayer. Don't ask questions: Wait for hope to appear. (Lamentations 3:25-29, MSG)

Just Suppose

Just suppose, when I pray, there really is
someone listening who cares about me
and wants to know what is on my mind.

Just suppose, when I pray, it changes me
and my view of how the universe
operates and who is involved.

Just suppose, I put my doubts aside for a
minute and consider the possibility that
someone who knew me before I was
born loves me, warts and all, without
condition or reservation, no matter how
badly I have behaved in the past.

Just suppose, a prayer was my first response
instead of my last resort when facing a
new challenge or an old temptation.

Just suppose, I lived each day, knowing
that there is an inexhaustible supply of
love for me to pass along to others.

—Phil Hodges

PRAYING FOR OUR KIDS

As parents, it's important that we pray for ourselves and our role, so we can be better servant leaders at home. But it's also important to pray for our children.

Phil Hodges, for instance, found great joy in praying for the future spouses of his children from the time they were little. He prayed that they would be growing in homes where the love of Jesus and love of one another was being taught. When his son-in-law and daughter-in-law turned out to be kids he already knew, he delighted in telling them that he'd been praying for them for more than twenty years.

After praying about it—what a concept!—I came up with four foundational things to pray for my children daily. Yes, there are things to add, but this is a great place to start. To make these things easier to remember, think of the children's praise song "Head and Shoulders, Knees and Toes."

Head: Pray your children will always lift their heads to look to the Lord, and when they're too hurt or discouraged, pray they'll allow God to lift their heads.

> *But you, GOD, shield me on all sides; you ground my feet,*
> *you lift my head high. (Psalm 3:3, MSG)*

Shoulders: Pray your children will learn to let God carry their burdens.

> *Pile your troubles on GOD's shoulders—he'll carry your load,*
> *he'll help you out. (Psalm 55:22, MSG)*

Knees: Pray your children will get on their knees before God often.

> *Purify your inner life. Quit playing the field. Hit bottom, and*
> *cry your eyes out. The fun and games are over. Get serious,*
> *really serious. Get down on your knees before the Master;*
> *it's the only way you'll get on your feet. (James 4:8-10, MSG)*

Toes: Pray your kids will be connected to a community of believers who will keep them on their toes.

So watch your step, friends. Make sure there's no evil unbelief lying around that will trip you up and throw you off course, diverting you from the living God. For as long as it's still God's Today, keep each other on your toes so sin doesn't slow down your reflexes. If we can only keep our grip on the sure thing we started out with, we're in this with Christ for the long haul. (Hebrews 3:12-14, MSG)

If you like this list, share it with a friend. Can you see all of us around the world praying for our children as we sing, "Head and shoulders, knees and toes, knees and toes, knees and toes . . ."?

Pause & Reflect

- **If you couldn't pray about your children's safety, health, happiness, or success in school or extracurricular activities, what would be your most frequent prayers for them? Why?**

"BUT I'M SO BUSY . . ."

Studying Scripture reinforces your habits of solitude and prayer. If you want time to study God's Word but don't find it possible with little ones, here are seven ideas that have helped me to parent more like Jesus by drawing me closer to Him.

1. *Have Scripture e-mailed to you.* For many years I read through the Bible on a reading plan. This site has plans that are e-mailed to you: http://www.biblegateway.com/resources/readingplans/.

You can choose to read the whole Bible through the year, but I'd recommend starting with the New Testament first. Also, if you get behind, don't let the e-mails pile up. Delete the old ones and get back on track. It's about reading God's Word and spending time with Jesus. No guilt allowed!

2. *Keep a Bible open on the kitchen counter.* Yes, it might acquire spaghetti sauce stains, but I don't think Jesus will mind. If it's there and open you can read God's Word and whisper thoughts and prayers to Him as the bread is toasting or the pasta is boiling. God's ears are attuned to kitchen prayers just as much as ones whispered on your knees on a quiet morning.

3. *Watch Christian sermons on the Internet.* Some of my favorites are videos of Francis Chan and Beth Moore. I've pulled them up on my computer while I'm folding clothes instead of turning on *Good Morning America* or *The View*—much more uplifting!

4. *Keep a devotional book in your bathroom.* One of my recent favorites is *Nothing Is Impossible: A Women of Faith Devotional* (Thomas Nelson, 2010). I've discovered I can read a devotion and meditate on the Scripture verse in the time it takes to blow-dry my hair.

5. *Have a Bible study time with your kids.* For years I used Keys for Kids (http://www.cbhministries.org/ForKids/KeysforKids/ReadListen.aspx). It's online and it's *free*. The best part was that the kids loved it, and they kept me accountable!

6. *Ask your spouse to be your Bible reading partner.* About seven years ago John and I started reading the Bible together before he leaves for work. We're reading through the Bible, but we don't try to stick to a plan. We tried that and it just stressed us out!

Instead, we keep a bookmark in the Bible and pick up where we left off last time. We each take a turn reading a chapter out loud if we have time. If not, we split a chapter and each read half. We don't stress if we can't get it in, but we enjoy it when we do. It also gives us great topics of conversation throughout the day.

7. *Join a Bible study.* I know this can be a challenge, but it can also be a great joy. I joined Bible Study Fellowship (http://www.bsfinternational.org) last year because it provides great studies and has an amazing children's program. Not only do moms get to hear God's Word; their children do, too.

There is weekly homework, but it takes only fifteen to twenty minutes a day, on average. I fit this in by waking up earlier than normal or by asking my husband to watch the toddler for a few minutes. It's hard for him to say no when I tell him I need to study the Bible!

Pause & Reflect

- Do you think parents need to read the Bible more than, less than, or the same amount as non-parents? Why?
- What Bible study ideas can you add to Tricia's list of seven?

TWELVE

Moving On

PRINCIPLE 12

To Lead Like Jesus, Turn Mistakes into Opportunities Through Forgiveness and Grace

As a parent, you'll encounter many mistakes—both your own and others'. Phil shows how the gifts of grace and forgiveness, two of Christ's specialties, can turn mistakes into opportunities for divine healing in your family.

The other day I watched two of my five-year-old grandsons getting into a spat on the playground. They were playing tag; one pushed the other a little too hard, knocking him down.

There was an immediate shout of discontent from the injured party: "Samuel, I don't like you anymore!"

With that, the boys walked away from each other with unhappy faces. Several minutes passed. The boys avoided one another, looking a little lonesome. As I watched, their angry expressions slowly melted, and they started looking at each other out of the corners of their eyes.

As an interested spectator, I was hoping to see an apology offered and accepted. What happened next was even better. The boys became interested in what some other kids were doing and raced off together, chattering as if the incident had never happened.

In that moment I saw what the fruit of forgiveness is supposed to be—and how profoundly it could affect the families we love and lead.

Pause & Reflect

- "And [Jesus] said: 'I tell you the truth, unless you change and become like little children, you will never enter the kingdom of heaven. Therefore, whoever humbles himself like this child is the greatest in the kingdom of heaven'" (Matthew 18:3-4). If you became more like a child when it comes to forgiveness, what might that look like?

AS WE FORGIVE OUR DEBTORS

When we're kids, we live in the moment. A small offense remains that way—small. Yet as we grow older, the list of hurts and disappointments grows longer and our ability to hold grudges grows stronger.

For parents, as for everyone else, forgiveness requires intentional surrender. It demands that we leave the debts—for which our pride and ego demand payment—uncollected.

As we guide our children through the long, slow process to maturity, we need to be open to learning lessons from them, too. We need forgiveness and grace to be active habits and parts of our leadership. We need to extend forgiveness and grace to our children, and to other people who may offend us on our parenting journey: teachers, coaches, other parents, and even grandparents.

More than that, we often need to extend forgiveness to ourselves. You will mess up as a person and a parent—all of us do. Instead of dwelling on our failures, we need to pick ourselves up, brush ourselves off, turn to God to help us with our pride and ego, and forgive ourselves for not being perfect. God doesn't expect our perfection—and we shouldn't, either. But He does expect—and require—forgiveness.

Unlike Jesus, we all fall short of 100 percent in our journey as leaders. This is especially true in our role as parents. Sometimes we make mistakes that could have been avoided. Sometimes we say or do things in the heat of the moment that we regret. If our egos are wrapped up in our performance and the opinions of others, we'll be unable to forgive our own shortcomings—let alone anyone else's.

An unforgiving heart is not capable of leading like Jesus at home or anywhere else. It will always look backward to justify not moving forward in a relationship. An unforgiving heart stores up resentment and marinates in bitterness. It's stingy with praise and microscopic in its judgment and suspicion of others. It will isolate its owner and cause him or her to wear the attitude of a martyr or victim in dealing with others.

Leaders seeking to grow and develop people need a healthy capacity to forgive, correct, and move on. As family leaders, we can be sure that everyone we deal with, including ourselves, is going to make mistakes or otherwise disappoint us.

Forgiveness is not a natural response when someone hurts you or your children, or fails to meet expectations. But forgiveness is what Jesus calls us to as an extension of what He did for us on the cross.

Forgiveness is at the core of our relationship with God. We can engage in the supernatural act of forgiving because we've been forgiven through the blood of Jesus Christ. Forgiveness is the way for a heart grounded in the unconditional love of God to respond to the imperfections of others.

Forgiveness is a hallmark of what it means to lead like Jesus. He taught it to His disciples, and He practiced it toward those who betrayed Him. He grants forgiveness willingly to those who accept the gift of His sacrifice.

By practicing grace and forgiveness, we can create harmony in our homes. When we forgive with grace, we model the essence of what Jesus was all about. Nowhere was this more evident than on the cross, when He said this:

> *"Father, forgive them, for they do not know*
> *what they are doing." (Luke 23:34)*

Pause & Reflect

- "For if you forgive men when they sin against you, your heavenly Father will also forgive you. But if you do not forgive men their sins, your Father will not forgive your sins" (Matthew 6:14-15). Is forgiveness a suggestion or a command? Why is it easier to believe it to be a suggestion at times?
- Do you think most family members forgive each other more readily, less readily, or about the same as people in general do? Why?

THE PENALTY BOX

When a player commits a personal foul in ice hockey, he's sent to sit in the penalty box for a specific amount of time depending on the severity of the infraction. During that time the team continues to play short-handed without access to the skills and creativity of the player.

This happens in families, too. Sometimes we put people in the penalty box when they've hurt or disappointed us.

This can happen without the other person even knowing it. Rather than going through painful confrontation and exposing our own vulnerability, we pull away and privately put the offender in the penalty box. The big problem is that we don't place a time limit on how long we keep the person there. When this happens, we go about our business a little sadder and feeling like we're living life short-handed. Not only does unforgiveness hurt our relationships, it poisons us inside as we hold it in.

Many of us don't understand what forgiveness is all about. It's not forgetting or dismissing the impact of a wrong. It's choosing not to let that wrong dominate the future of your life and relationships. Forgiveness is "giving" the infraction to God. It's as if we're saying, "Here You go, Father; this is no longer my concern. Please take care of the matter in Your wisdom and according to Your will."

Roadblocks to Forgiveness

Here are just a few:

- a parent-teacher conference that exposes shortcomings in your parenting
- a coach who doesn't let your child play as much as you think she should
- an unintentional injury to one of your children
- gossip and misinformation spread with malice
- violated rules of morality and ethics
- favoritism in selection processes at school or other activities

All these events can become live battlegrounds over whether we Edge God Out and respond in anger and resentment—or Exalt God Only and extend grace and forgiveness.

The price of forgiveness is letting go of the need to receive an apology or repayment for a wrong. If you hold on to either as a precondition of forgiveness, you'll never have an unhindered heart.

You may understand all this, but inside you still may be fighting it: "I know it's what I'm supposed to do, but I can't do it in my own strength." The good news is God doesn't ask you to. Instead, He asks that you simply share your desire to forgive, and surrender to Him your unwillingness to forgive.

Create in me a pure heart, O God, and renew
a steadfast spirit within me. (Psalm 51:10)

What happens when we ask God to make forgiveness possible in us? The reward is a heart freed of bitterness. There is also the potential of restored relationship and new hope and joy for the future! What could be better than that?

In the encouraging words sent to me recently by a friend, "The one who apologizes first is the bravest. The one who forgives first is the strongest. The one who forgets first is the happiest."

There is never a good reason to forfeit peace and freedom to an unforgiving heart. Will you turn to God today to help you be a brave, strong, and happy family leader? He wants that.

It's from a place of freedom and truth that we lead our children best. If you need help, you know the One to speak to. He's just a prayer away.

Pause & Reflect

- Are there family members, alive or dead, you've been keeping in the penalty box? Speak their names out loud. In a prayer of surrender, turn over the penalty box keys to the One who'll lead you in the process of forgiveness.
- Have you ever tried to put God in the penalty box because of a specific hurt or disappointment? Is He still there? If so, what do you want to tell Him?
- Is there something you've done as a parent that's caused you to withhold forgiveness from yourself, even though you've been forgiven by God? Isn't it time to open the door to the penalty box and be free?

DON'T JUST SAY GRACE

One definition of grace is "unmerited favor." I love that definition, don't you?

Imagine you've been rightly convicted of a crime and have been brought before the judge to determine your fine. If the judge gives you the fine you deserve, that will be justice. If the judge gives you a fine that's less than you deserve, that will be mercy.

If the judge comes down from the bench and offers to pay the full fine himself, that will be grace.

For it is by grace you have been saved, through faith—
and this not from yourselves, it is the gift of God—not by works,
so that no one can boast. (Ephesians 2:8-9)

It's the grace that God extended to us through the blood of His beloved Son that calls us, in gratitude, to give grace to others and teach our children to do the same. Sometimes we may feel we have a good reason not to extend grace, but this equation reveals the truth:

Grace + Anything Else = Anything but Grace

There's no excuse not to offer grace to others, including those we lead in our families. That's because of another truth:

While we were still sinners, Christ died for us.
(Romans 5:8)

It was about fifty-five years ago, but I remember clearly the day my mother sent me out to the garage to speak to my father. I'd broken curfew the night before and was caught in a lie about where I'd been. Mom was furious, and rightfully so, about my misconduct. She was turning me over to Dad for a just punishment.

Things didn't look good when my dad told me to close the garage door. Without turning from the work he was doing, he asked if Mom's report on what I'd purportedly done was true. I reluctantly confessed that it was.

Dad was an emotional man, and I could sense his anger rising as the full story of what I'd done was disclosed. He still hadn't turned around when I finished my account. I wasn't sure what form my punishment would take, but expected the worst. I knew I would deserve it.

I hoped for mercy, but didn't receive it. What I got was grace.

Dad turned around. I don't know what it was about the expression I had on my face, but something struck him as funny. I must have looked so pitiful and remorseful that he couldn't sustain his anger. He burst out laughing.

Finally he told me that I'd been a real bonehead. He made me promise never to pull a stupid move like that again. I quickly and wholeheartedly gave him my word.

This scene of grace was completed when we walked out of the garage, arm in arm. Dad not only accepted me; he would also absorb the full force of my mother's unhappiness with him for letting me off the hook.

That day bore sweet fruit years later when I extended grace to my dad concerning a decision he'd made that threatened our relationship. This time I was the one who let him off the hook. We again got through it together, walking arm in arm. That reflects, I think, still another truth about what happens when we teach our kids to practice forgiveness and grace:

> *Train a child in the way he should go, and when he is old*
> *he will not turn from it. (Proverbs 22:6)*

MOVING BEYOND MISTAKES

Grace-filled family leadership is all about turning mistakes into opportunities for growth. Jesus modeled this when, after His resurrection, He encountered Peter—who three times had denied even knowing Jesus after the latter's arrest. It could have been a humiliating rejection for Peter, but Jesus made sure it wasn't. Here's what happened:

> When Simon Peter realized that it was the Master, he threw on some clothes, for he was stripped for work, and dove into the sea. The other disciples came in by boat for they weren't far from land, a hundred yards or so, pulling along the net full of fish. When they got out of the boat, they saw a fire laid, with fish and bread cooking on it. . . .
>
> Jesus said, "Breakfast is ready." Not one of the disciples dared ask, "Who are you?" They knew it was the Master.
>
> Jesus then took the bread and gave it to them. He did the same with

the fish. This was now the third time Jesus had shown himself alive to the disciples since being raised from the dead.

After breakfast, Jesus said to Simon Peter, "Simon, son of John, do you love me more than these?"

"Yes, Master, you know I love you."

Jesus said, "Feed my lambs."

He then asked a second time, "Simon, son of John, do you love me?"

"Yes, Master, you know I love you."

Jesus said, "Shepherd my sheep."

Then he said it a third time: "Simon, son of John, do you love me?"

Peter was upset that he asked for the third time, "Do you love me?" so he answered, "Master, you know everything there is to know. You've got to know that I love you."

Jesus said, "Feed my sheep. I'm telling you the very truth now. When you were young you dressed yourself and went wherever you wished, but when you get old you'll have to stretch out your hands while someone else dresses you and takes you where you don't want to go." He said this to hint at the kind of death by which Peter would glorify God. And then he commanded, "Follow me." (John 21:7-9, 12-19, MSG)

Instead of dressing Peter down or giving him the silent treatment, Jesus restored him to service. We need to do the same with our children. It's easy to say, but hard to do—especially when you see one of your kids make a very costly mistake.

I remember one such time when my son, who was then in his twenties, dropped out of law school. It could have been a defining moment—in a bad way. My response could have set him up for failure.

But I helped him step back and say, "There's a lesson to be learned here." Yes, a lot of money had been spent in an unsuccessful venture, but maybe some life lessons could be learned from the experience.

"What positive things did you learn about yourself from law school?" I asked him. He said he learned he could work hard and that he was smart enough to do the work. He shared other positive things, too.

I then asked, "What could you have done differently?"

He replied that when he received feedback on his performance, he didn't use the information well. When he did better on a test than he expected, he celebrated; when he received what he expected, he didn't investigate it further. If he got a lower-than-expected grade, he didn't go back to the teacher and ask what he could have done better. Instead of talking to the people who were grading the papers to find out how to be successful, he consulted his friends. In the end they were not a reliable source of the advice or help he needed.

We talked about communication, pride, starting new projects, tackling the routine parts of a job before the exciting parts, not majoring in minors, and seeking feedback.

Perhaps someday you'll need to help your child work through an expensive life lesson. If so, remember that disappointments may be God's appointments to draw us closer to Him. While we want to protect our children from hardship, that's impossible. Instead, we may be called to lead by walking them gracefully through the valley and guiding them through the shadows.

Pause & Reflect

- In the short term, is it more satisfying to lecture a child who's made a mistake, or to help him or her gain insight from that mistake? How about in the long term?
- To follow the advice in this chapter, which of the following would help you most: patience, remembering your own mistakes, having a spouse or friend to whom you can vent frustrations, or trusting God with your children's futures? How can you rely on God to help you develop in these areas?

BEING THERE

To extend grace and forgiveness to our kids, of course, we need to be there in the first place. I remember many days from long ago when I missed being there for my kids. And I thank God for their mother, who tried to make up the difference.

One of the greatest gifts we can give our children is time. This goes for both parents, though many dads—like me—have had particular problems in this area. As primary models of fatherhood, dads are called to pass on the grace we receive from our heavenly Father. This means being present not only physically, but also actively listening to the desires of our children's hearts and understanding what's going on in their world.

Being a loving role model means teaching children by example, helping them figure out what's important, and showing them how to do the little things all kids need to know. Most importantly, we must share the grace of our presence. Doing this sends the most important message every child wants to hear: "You are special, son. You are loved, daughter. You are a treasure to me." Those tender messages will propel them as no other along the path they should go.

If these messages go undelivered, it will create a longing that lasts a lifetime. Just ask someone who walks through life with that hole in his or her heart that only a parent—often a father—can fill.

If you don't want your kids hiding from you or disregarding you when they get older, be there for them now. Be there when they need you and when they hunger for your company. If you don't, someday they might decide they don't want you there at all.

When we're present for one another, a relationship is built. It won't be perfect, but hopefully it will be one where we can accept and extend forgiveness and grace.

Whatever season of life you're in, it's never too late to reach out with encouragement and love to your children. It's never too early to be there for them.

Pause & Reflect

- What message do you think today's parents—especially dads—need to hear most? What message do you most want to get into your kids' hearts?
- What do you need to do more of to deliver the "grace of presence" to your children?
- What do you need to *stop* doing in order to be "in the moment" with your children while you still have the opportunity?

I want to get in my kids' hearts how much God loves them, and how precious they are to Him. Not only the way most churches teach today. But deep down, if they can understand their worth in His eyes, it will change how they see themselves, how they allow Him to be the Lord of their life because He deserves that place.

—ALLISON, mother of three

I want my kids to understand most that God created us in His image. He doesn't ever want to tarnish that image, nor let it go astray. Prayer, meditation, and reading of His Word should be our first response to how to live and lead in a godly way. He will never leave us or forsake us if we choose to follow Him. He will always be our greatest teacher, cheerleader, and ever-present counselor. If you have God, you have everything you need.

—JENNIFER, mother of two

My biggest challenge in being connected and staying connected with my children is busyness. I am busy most of the time. I have five children, a job, and a household to run. Things need to be done. People don't eat

or have clean clothes if I don't do my work. But I also have things that
I choose to keep me busy. The Internet is my busyness of choice. It sucks
time away from my family and it is a busyness that I don't "have" to do.
I choose it.

—MICHELLE, mother of five

SURPRISED BY GRACE

One Sunday morning several years ago I was standing at the front of the worship center in our church, ready to pray with people at the conclusion of the service. This was one of the pleasant functions of being a church elder that I normally enjoyed. On this particular morning, however, I was not in a very joyful mood. I'd been experiencing a major case of writer's block on a book, and was frustrated with my lack of progress. When no one approached me to pray, I was secretly relieved.

Just as I was about to quit my post, a shy-looking teenage girl with a mouthful of braces approached. She told me her name was Angie, and asked if I would pray about her coming week at school. I said I'd be happy to, and asked what was it about the week that she wanted me to pray for.

Angie said she was having problems with some of the kids at school and wasn't sure how to handle it. She also mentioned a big book report that was due, which she was having trouble completing. With this information we bowed our heads and I prayed that the Lord would provide Angie with wisdom and courage to respond to friends in a loving way, that she'd be able to focus on her report, and that she'd be able to finish it on time and do a good job.

I thought our time together was about to end. But instead of returning to her seat, Angie looked at me with a smile. "Can I pray for you?"

The question took me by surprise. I'd been prepared to give support and encouragement, but wasn't expecting to receive it.

"Yes," I replied. "I would like that very much."

"What is it that I can pray for?" she asked.

"Well, I am writing a book and right now I'm stuck. I can't get what I want to say down on paper. I could use some prayer to help me get back on track."

"Sure." As we bowed our heads, Angie prayed in the most natural way: "Please God, please help Mr. Phil get unstuck. He looks like he has a lot on his mind and could use Your help writing it down. In Jesus' name, amen."

"Thank you," I said.

"Anytime," she answered with her metallic smile. As she turned to leave, her grin was even bigger. "I'll be praying for you this week. 'Bye."

Amazement washed over me. What a good God to use a teenager with a mouthful of braces to bless me when I least expected it.

For me, the meaning of that moment has continued to build as an example of the gift of grace.

By being in the moment, accepting each other's differences, and engaging in mutual encouragement, we can offer grace to one another anytime, anyplace—even in our families.

Pause & Reflect

- Which of the following do you most need to do as a first step toward extending grace to your family? Quieting yourself to be "in the moment" with Him? Or with each family member? Accepting the fact that in all His holiness He still wants you to come to Him just as you are? Trusting in His unconditional love as the reason behind all He asks of you as a parent?
- What would you like to ask or tell Him about this? Won't you pray about it now?

Dear Lord,
Thank You for Your compassion, mercy, faithfulness, and goodness. Teach
me to wait quietly on You during trials in my life. Know that my hope is in

You, even when my mouth and actions go against that. Teach me to be
mindful of Your words about love never failing (1 Corinthians 13:4-8)
when I see my children each morning, each day, and before they sleep
for the night. Thank You for Your unconditional love and the family that
has been trusted to me. Remind me daily that "to whom much is given,
much is required" so that I may grow Your kingdom one family member
at a time. Help me to do my best in that. Give me no more than I can
handle, help me be a voice for You in my words, actions, and thoughts.
Amen!

—JENNIFER, mother of two

TIME TO FOLLOW THE LEADER

Jesus was a model for "being in the moment." I don't think training His disciples was a hit-and-miss thing. Since Jesus was intentional about all He did on earth, the leading of the men closest to Him was no doubt done with thoughtfulness and an understanding that can only come from a heaven-sent vision. As He walked together with His disciples on the journey of life, Jesus observed them in the moment, listened to them, and answered their questions.

I'd like to think that the time Jesus spent walking to and from work alongside His earthly father, Joseph, resting in the midday for a meal with him, and asking him questions helped to prepare Jesus to offer the same kind of relaxed fellowship to His disciples. Like father, like son—in more ways than one.

That doesn't just apply *then*, but also *now*. Remember what Jesus said:

> **"For where two or three come together in my name,**
> **there am I with them." (Matthew 18:20)**

The grace of Jesus' presence can be with us today. Two thousand years after He walked on earth, His beckoning voice still calls, saying, "Come to Me," and "Abide in Me."

As I described at the beginning of this chapter, young children live fully in the moment. They aren't thinking of the past or looking toward the future. Crying, skipping, or jumping up and down, they live in a real-time world and hunger for you to be there with them.

One of my favorite images of a parent in the moment with a child is my sister-in-law, Susanne, talking with her children when they were young. Because of a hearing loss, it's a challenge for her to understand what people are saying unless they're faced directly toward her.

So whenever her little ones wanted to speak with her, Susanne would kneel down, lovingly hold their face with both hands, and listen with her eyes and ears to what they had to say. It's a beautiful picture of listening that we can incorporate into our parenting.

I also like to think of Jesus doing the same thing as we turn to Him for help. Can you picture the tenderness in His eyes? Can you imagine His desire to lead you with tender care?

Leading your family like Jesus starts with being led by Jesus. Being led by Jesus is all about turning to Him, following Him, and knowing He's not only walking beside you on your journey as a parent; He's doing so with tender, loving care.

Pause & Reflect

- How can you approach your day differently to find the right balance between meeting your child's need for your attention and your reality of being overwhelmed?
- If you could turn to Jesus and look into His eyes right now, what do you think He'd say to you as a parent? What would you say to Him?
- As you prepare to lead your family like Jesus, which of the principles in this book do you most want to remember?

I have to remember that some things can wait. My children are growing like weeds and I don't want to miss a moment with them. I want to enjoy every one!

—KENNISHA, mother of three

I often get caught up in all that needs to be done, instead of just taking the time to be in the moment with [my kids]. I try to be intentional about being sure to look them in the eyes whenever I can. Sounds like a little thing, but with all the multi-tasking that us moms do, I'm usually talking to my kids while I'm answering an e-mail, cooking lunch, or folding laundry. So I try to be aware of them more, look them in the eyes when we're talking, and take every opportunity to give them a hug and a smooch!

—DIANE, mother of two

Points to Ponder about the *Habits* of Leading Like Jesus as a Parent

- Have you decided to parent like Jesus? If so, have you developed the necessary habits to stay the course no matter what the circumstances?

- The key is remembering that Jesus stayed on track with His mission by applying five habits that countered the negative forces working against Him:
    1. Solitude
    2. Prayer
    3. Studying and applying Scripture
    4. Accepting and responding to God's unconditional love
    5. Involvement in supportive relationships

- Adapting the same habits is essential for parents who seek to follow Jesus as their role model for leadership with their kids.

- Forgiveness and grace are indispensable ingredients of leading your family like Jesus.

FINAL THOUGHTS

Now you know that leading your family like Jesus is about transforming your *heart, head, hands*, and *habits*.

As you apply the concepts you've learned in this book, remember that parenting like Jesus is a daily journey and challenge rather than a final destination. This journey will always be filled with failures, roughly-right behaviors, and out-and-out victories. To keep on keeping on, we suggest two strategies:

First, pray constantly. Ask God to guide you to the truth that will have the greatest impact on improving the way you parent.

Second, periodically review your progress in leading your family like Jesus. Celebrate it, and redirect your efforts when you think you've lapsed.

You'll be surprised what God will do through you as you apply these biblical principles to your parenting. If you want a true picture of how well you're making positive changes, watch the reactions your younger kids have to you. As they get older, ask them for feedback: What's working—and what's not?

To serve your children as Christ serves us means honoring God and His commandments and putting the love of Jesus into your parenting. When you do that, you'll leave a positive legacy for your children, their children, and their children's children.

Trust Jesus as your parenting leadership role model. When you do, you'll make Him smile—and help your children fulfill their heaven-sent potential.

May God bless you on your parenting journey!

ABOUT THE AUTHORS

KEN BLANCHARD, coauthor of *The One Minute Manager®* and more than fifty other management and leadership books, is widely characterized as one of the most insightful, powerful, and compassionate people in business today. He is known for his knack for making the seemingly complex easy to understand. Ken is chief spiritual officer of The Ken Blanchard Companies™, a global leader in workplace learning, employee productivity, leadership, and team effectiveness. He cofounded the company with Margie Blanchard, his wife of fifty years. Their children, Scott and Debbie, have played major roles in making The Ken Blanchard Companies the most admired firm in its industry. Ken, along with Phil Hodges, is also the cofounder of Lead Like Jesus, a nonprofit ministry.

PHIL HODGES, a lifelong friend of Ken Blanchard, served as a human resource and industrial relations manager in corporate America for thirty-six years with Xerox Corporation and U.S. Steel.

During his career at Xerox, Phil served as chief negotiator for fifty collective bargaining agreements and as the senior human resources manager for a thousand-employee manufacturing operation.

As chairman of his local church elder council for six years, Phil developed a passion for bringing effective leadership principles into the life of the local church. He and his family served on short-term mission projects both in the USA and internationally. In 1999, Phil and Ken cofounded Lead Like Jesus where Phil has served as its first managing director and as chief content officer. He and Ken Blanchard have coauthored five books: *Lead Like Jesus: Lessons from the Greatest Leadership Role Model of All Time; The Most Loving Place in Town: A Modern Day Parable for the Church; Leadership Development for Every Day of the Year; The Servant Leader;* and *Leadership by the Book* (with Bill Hybels). Phil and his wife, Jane Kinnaird Hodges, live in southern California, where they enjoy daily interaction and involvement in the lives of their two married children, their children's spouses, and seven grandchildren.

TRICIA GOYER is a bestselling author of more than thirty novels, including *Night Song*, which was awarded American Christian Fiction Writers' 2005 Book of the Year for Long Historical Romance, and *Dawn of a Thousand Nights*, which won the same award in 2006. Her coauthored novel *The Swiss Courier* was a Christy Award nominee. She has also authored nine nonfiction books and more than three hundred articles for national publications. In 2003, Tricia was one of two authors named "Writer of the Year" at the Mount Hermon Christian Writer's Conference, and she has been interviewed by *Focus on the Family*, *Moody Midday Connection*, *The Harvest Show*, *NBC's Monday Today*, *Aspiring Women*, and hundreds of other radio and television programs. Tricia and her husband, John, have four children and one grandchild and live in Arkansas.

LOOKING FOR YOUR
NEXT STEPS?

Parent or pastor, CEO or teacher, shopkeeper or student—if you want to influence others by leading like Jesus, join the Lead Like Jesus movement and expand your leadership abilities. We offer leadership-building resources for everyone—from moms and dads to teens to young adults to seasoned executives—all with the goal of demonstrating God's love for people while helping them change the way they live, love, and lead.

MAKE SURE TO TURN THE PAGE...
TO LEARN MORE ABOUT OUR PRODUCTS!

Visit us online to purchase the following resources at
www.LeadLikeJesus.com

 LEAD LIKE JESUS

E-DEVOTIONS

Sign up to receive a brief, insightful, challenging reflection three times a week in your inbox—a great way to learn more about leading like Jesus.

LLJ STUDY GUIDES

Continue your personal growth with principles, activities, memory verses, and prayers for creating your own leadership plan.

STUDENT RESOURCES

These materials start early, developing leadership habits and skills that will last a lifetime.

ATTEND AN ENCOUNTER

This interactive, high-impact program helps leaders create positive change in their personal and professional relationships.

ACCELERATE™

Built to move at a speed that's right for you, this daily online program blends reading, video, and powerful questions to foster continued growth as an LLJ leader.

All products are available to purchase at
www.LeadLikeJesus.com

FOCUS ON THE FAMILY®

Welcome to the Family

Whether you purchased this book, borrowed it, or received it as a gift, thanks for reading it! This is just one of many insightful, biblically based resources that Focus on the Family produces for people in all stages of life.

Focus is a global Christian ministry dedicated to helping families thrive as they celebrate and cultivate God's design for marriage and experience the adventure of parenthood. Our outreach exists to support individuals and families in the joys and challenges they face, and to equip and empower them to be the best they can be.

Through our many media outlets, we offer help and hope, promote moral values and share the life-changing message of Jesus Christ with people around the world.

Focus on the Family MAGAZINES

These faith-building, character-developing publications address the interests, issues, concerns, and challenges faced by every member of your family from preschool through the senior years.

For More INFORMATION

ONLINE:
Log on to
FocusOnTheFamily.com
In Canada, log on to
FocusOnTheFamily.ca

PHONE:
Call toll-free:
**800-A-FAMILY
(232-6459)**
In Canada, call toll-free:
800-661-9800

THRIVING FAMILY®
Marriage & Parenting

FOCUS ON THE FAMILY CLUBHOUSE JR.®
Ages 4 to 8

FOCUS ON THE FAMILY CLUBHOUSE®
Ages 8 to 12

FOCUS ON THE FAMILY CITIZEN®
U.S. news issues

Rev. 3/11

More expert resources
for marriage and parenting . . .

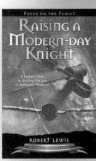
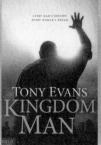
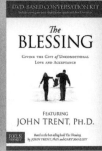

Do you want to be a better parent? Enjoy a stronger marriage? Focus on the Family's collection of inspiring, practical resources can help your family grow closer and stronger than ever before. Whichever format you might need—video, audio, book or e-book, we have something for you. Visit our online Family Store and discover how we can help your family thrive at **FocusOnTheFamily.com/resources**.